THE SECRET BATTLE

A. P. Herbert

THE
SECRET BATTLE
A Tragedy of the First World War

WITH A FOREWORD
BY
SIR WINSTON CHURCHILL

INTRODUCTION BY MALCOLM BROWN

Frontline Books, London

The Secret Battle: A Tragedy of the First World War

This edition published in 2009 by Frontline Books,
an imprint of Pen & Swords Books Limited,
47 Church Street, Barnsley, S. Yorkshire, S70 2AS
www.frontline-books.com

ISBN: 978-1-84832-521-0

Publishing History

The Secret Battle was first published in 1919 by
Methuen & Co Ltd, London. Subsequent editions have been
published by Brown Watson Ltd (London, 1963); Chatto & Windus
(London, 1970); Hutchinson (London,1976); Oxford University Press
(Oxford, 1982); and House of Stratus (Cornwall, 2001).

A CIP data record for this title is available from the British Library.

For more information on our books, please visit
www.frontline-books.com, email info@frontline-books.com
or write to us at the above address.

Printed by the MPG Books Group in the UK

FOREWORD

BY

Sir Winston Churchill

THIS story of a valiant heart tested to destruction took rank when it was first published a few months after the Armistice, as one of the most moving of the novels produced by the war. It was at that time a little swept aside by the revulsion of the public mind from anything to do with the awful period just ended. But on re-reading it nine years later it seems to hold its place, and indeed a permanent place, in war literature. It was one of those cries of pain wrung from the fighting troops by the prolonged and measureless torment through which they passed; and like the poems of Siegfried Sasson should be read in each generation, so that men and women may rest under no illusion about what war means. In 1919 it was first and foremost a chronicle valued for the sober truth of its descriptions and its narration of what might happen to a gallant soldier borne down by stresses incredible to those who have not endured them, and caught in the steel teeth of the military machine.

The tale is founded on fact. Nevertheless, as the writer has been careful to make clear, it is not an authentic account. All the facts on which it rests happened, and many of them happened in combination to a very large number of young men who fought for us or who fought against us, and to those who loved them. But they did not all happen to the same man ; or in so far as they fell upon one individual, the emphasis and setting were not the same. It can now be judged from a more detached, and in some respects more exacting, standpoint as a work of art. It is a monument of the agony, not of one but of millions, standing impassive in marble to give its message to all wayfarers who pass it. It speaks to the uninformed, to the unimaginative, to the headstrong, and to the short-memoried folk who need a word of warning on their path. It speaks also with that strange note of consolation, often underlying tragedy, to those who know only too well and can never forget. To a new generation of ardent, virile youth it can do no harm. They will not be deterred by its story from doing their duty by their native land, if ever the need should come. They will face terrors and tortures, if need be, with the simple faith that "What man has done, man can do". Nothing but good can come in future years to those older people—if such there be— who contemplate in sluggish acquiescence and airy detachment wars in which they will themselves bear no part. And piercing Complacency with barbed dart, it drives home the bitter invocation :

"Pray you'll never know
    The hell where youth and laughter go."

The author, who himself passed not unscathed but undaunted through much and some of the worst of what he describes, develops his tale with the measured fatefulness of a Greek tragedy. But here the pathos is all the greater because there is no element of Nemesis. The hero-victim is never anything but modest and dutiful : he always tries his best to do his bit. It is only the cruelty of chance which finally puts his life and his honour in the hands of the two men whose vanity he had offended. He had much to give. He gave it all. But a blind Fate declared it was not enough.

The restraint with which the author bridles his mercilessly gathered argument at every stage enables him to produce the climax in the very lowest key; and the reader is left to bear or express his own feelings as best he may. It is a soldier's tale cut in stone to melt all hearts.

INTRODUCTION

BY

MALCOLM BROWN

A.P. HERBERT was a prolific writer, a noted wit and a prominent public personality famous over many decades. Born in 1890, he was educated at Winchester and New College, Oxford, and it was from Oxford that he enlisted in response to the mood of the hour in the summer of 1914. Beginning as a lowly Ordinary Seaman in the Royal Navy, he was shortly commissioned as a Sub Lieutenant, though he found himself destined not to serve at sea but on land as a member of the newly created Royal Naval Division, a product of the inventive genius of the First Lord of the Admiralty, none other than the dynamic Winston Churchill. Finding that even the world's largest navy could not cope with the flood of volunteers flocking to the flag in response to the nation's call, Churchill decided that naval personnel for whom there was no space in His

Majesty's ships should be turned into infantrymen. Having expected to be trained to cope with knots and splices and to be taught the rudiments of seamanship, instead they suddenly found themselves learning to fight with rifles. The new division's members were to retain their naval ranks, though most of them would have only the most tenuous of contacts with the sea. Herbert served with the division for most of the war until being wounded and invalided out in 1917. The Royal Naval Division won an honourable reputation; after a brave but failed attempt to save Antwerp from falling into German hands in October 1914, in which Herbert was not involved, it became a notable presence first at Gallipoli and then on the Western Front where, transmuted into the 63rd (Royal Naval) Division, it took part in most of the major battles fought there from late 1916 onwards.

After the war Herbert was called to the bar in the Inner Temple, but never practised as a lawyer, preferring instead to forge what would become effectively a lifelong career as a humorous writer. He had been writing for *Punch*, Britain's leading humorous magazine, since 1910, and in 1924 he joined its staff; altogether he contributed regularly to its columns for sixty years. Additionally he wrote volumes of verse, novels and what he called 'near novels', numerous works of non-fiction, pamphlets, books on law, anthologies and collections, plus a whole galaxy of plays and, especially, musicals. He was also a distinguished independent Member of Parliament, with a particular interest in reform of the marriage and divorce laws. He lived by the Thames in Hammersmith, west London, and conceived a great love for the river and for sailing. In the Second World War he enlisted for the second time and became a petty officer in the Royal Naval (Thames) Patrol. At last, notionally at least, an awareness of knots and splices might have become useful. He was knighted in 1945 and in 1970 was appointed a Companion of Honour for 'services to literature'. He died, on the anniversary of Armistice Day, 11 November, in 1971.

Thus the basic facts. But the facts hardly do justice to the spirit and bravura of this extraordinary man. When in 1970 he published a sparkling autobiography to coincide with his eightieth birthday under the title *A.P.H.: His Life and Times*[1], his publishers, Messrs William Heinemann, included the following tribute in their blurb: 'There is more than a touch of the universal man about Alan Herbert – a great Englishman. Outspoken patriot, spirited denouncer of injustice, Bumbledom and humbug, tenacious defender of a good cause, he never loses his sense of fun – a *very* English attribute.'

The book here republished was A.P. Herbert's first, thrown off quickly in 1918 in the last months of the war. In a brief biographical note in an edition of the work published by Oxford University Press in 1982, it was stated: 'It will be seen that *The Secret Battle* was a highly uncharacteristic product.' That is indeed the case. There is not much humour in this book. On the contrary it is, literally, deadly serious. War was not really his subject, but one aspect of it caught his imagination and, evidently, fuelled a righteous anger which demanded that the story springing from that anger should be set down. Having made his case,

[1] Sir Alan Herbert, *A. P. H.: His Life and Times* (London: Heinemann, 1970)

having written his brilliant one-off parable, he left the subject alone. The war is only briefly referred to in his autobiography, with the notable exception that in the 1960s, in response to the mood and tone of the hugely popular musical and film *Oh! What a Lovely War*, he protested at the implication that men of his generation who had volunteered to fight for King and Country in 1914 had been fools and dupes. That was an interpretation he would not accept. They were men of honour and high duty who had firmly believed in their cause. More, having read in 'some young man's column' the allegation 'that the 1914 War was the most obscene and shameful act in our history', Herbert commented with some heat:

We had seen much that was obscene at Gallipoli, the Somme and Passchendaele, but nothing shameful. Would the war have been less shameful if we had lost it, if the British Fleet had steamed over to Heligoland to surrender or scuttle, if the people under British rule had been handed over to the gentle Germans? How I dislike these anaemic belittlers of our past!

The Secret Battle was published in 1919. Unlike many of his later writings, it was not a commercial success. Discussing it in his autobiography, he quipped: 'It was what Noel Coward, I think, would call a *flop d'estime*.'

He was right, initially, about the flop, but, he claimed, 'there was no doubt about the esteem'. Looking back from the perspective of today, we can now see it as a work of seminal importance. Its status as a contribution to the literature of the 1914–1918 War can be gauged by the fact that Field Marshal Montgomery, himself a veteran (indeed almost a fatality) of that conflict, called it 'the best story of front-line war I have read', while Winston Churchill wrote that it 'should be read in each generation, so that men and women may rest under no illusion about what war means'.

Yet such accolades immediately raise a question: why has this book not achieved the fame of the classic works about the 1914–1918 war that everybody has heard of? Why is it that most of those who bow at the shrines of such famous writers as Robert Graves or Siegfried Sassoon will almost certainly never have come across this brief but brilliant masterpiece?

The answer is, it might be thought, a curious one: it was written too soon. As Herbert himself put it, 'it was too early, too close to the War'. It was published in 1919, not many months after the Armistice, when the world was simply not ready for a book which cast disturbing shadows across a long and harrowing ordeal of which the prevailing view at that time was one of sheer overwhelming relief that it was over. In Churchill's words, *The Secret Battle* was 'swept aside by the revulsion of the public mind from anything to do with the awful period just ended'. The wounds were too painful, still raw, the bandages hardly applied. It was enough that the guns had fallen silent, that the newspapers no longer carried their massive daily casualty lists, that 'the boys', those who had survived, had at last 'come home', or at any rate were in process of doing so. A work not unlike a pebble thrown into a pool, with ripples raising doubts about certain sensitive aspects of the accepted military culture, was not in tune with the contemporary mood. It might almost have sunk without trace, had it not been retrieved by the good opinions of those who were not only moved by its story, but sensed its enduring value.

For now, ninety years after its first appearance, *The Secret Battle* might fairly be claimed to be more relevant to the prevailing attitudes, the current mood in relation to the whole concept of war, than it has ever been. Indeed, it is a tale whose hour, I believe, has finally come.

First, however, a word as to the book's title. Why the *secret* battle?

There had been any number of non-secret battles for the British public to take in over the previous four and more years when the book appeared in 1919. There had been four Battles of Ypres, two Battles of the Somme, other battles such as Loos in 1915 and Arras in 1917, and 1918 had been chock full of first German and then Allied offensives which were basically battles under other names. This is a book which is essentially about one young man's battle with himself, one young man's attempt to manage and come to terms with his own private war. Harry Penrose, the novel's central figure, tries his damndest to be equal to the challenges facing him, but, finally, fails. The outcome? He joins that small legion of men on the Western Front who were 'shot at dawn'. In the first paragraph of his book,

Herbert refers to 'Penrose's tragedy'. It is a bold word to use in a war which was, effectively, one long, sustained world tragedy. Responding to Herbert's interpretation, we have given this edition of the work a new subtitle. It might be deemed intrusive, indeed presumptuous, to call the book 'A Tragedy of the First World War', but, in addition to those which took place in that conflict, we have arguably had our fill of battles over the last ninety years. It is therefore, surely, necessary to fix this story against a background which present-day readers will immediately recognize and understand.

But to the nub of the book, its *raison d'être*. Where did Herbert find the subject matter which so perturbed him that he felt moved to put pen to paper in a field of literature to which he would never return?

The Secret Battle is a novel, but its source is a real event. It is a fiction woven about an actual non-fiction. You will not find the name of Harry Penrose among the lists of the fallen of the Great War, nor any indication of a known grave or a mention on one of the Western Front's many memorials, but there *was* a lookalike young officer of Penrose's vintage on whose story Herbert is presumed to have based his plot. The historic case in question was the execution of Sub Lieutenant Edwin Dyett, a junior officer in Herbert's own 63rd (Royal Naval) Division, following certain incidents in the late stages of the Battle of the Somme. He was court-martialled and sentenced to death, the sentence being duly carried out on 5 January 1917.

It is this central thrust of the story that makes this book so relevant to the climate of today. The subject of military executions has been much on the public mind in the early years of the new century. After an immensely long, highly emotional campaign, pardons have been granted to those men who were shot for cowardice or desertion during that war. The case, however, is far from closed. The arguments rage on. The public might, by and large, approve. The majority of historians do not. In this debate *The Secret Battle* is a not insignificant voice.

But how does the Dyett case relate to *The Secret Battle*?

The essential elements in the process that led to Dyett's execution are as follows:

On 13 November 1916 Herbert's 63rd

(Royal Naval) Division was ordered to take the village and railway station of Beaucourt in the Ancre valley in what was effectively the final thrust of the four-month-long Somme campaign. Sometime later that day, during a period of much uncertainty and confusion, Dyett and another officer were ordered to take command of a group of some two hundred men who were drifting rearwards from the lines and lead them back towards the fighting. Dyett demurred, not least because the officer who had given the order, a Sub Lieutenant Herring, was of the same rank as himself. Dyett allegedly replied: 'I find such chaos here that I think I had better go back and report to the Brigade.' Herring subsequently reported this exchange to the Staff Captain at Brigade Headquarters and the wheels of military justice began to revolve. A court martial was arranged and what had seemed at one point a relatively minor misdemeanour suddenly became serious. In Dyett's defence it was stated that he felt himself unfit to be an officer and had made four separate applications to transfer into the Navy or Royal Naval Reserve. His company commander was quoted as saying of him that 'his nerves prevented him from taking an active part in an advance' and that he had 'begged to be kept at base as he had not confidence in his powers of leadership'. However, a petty officer who had seen him on the day in question stated: 'Accused did not look as though he was afraid or in a funk. He looked as though he wanted to get out of it': a comment which, heavily underlined in the surviving court-martial papers, seems to have been seen as crucial to the case for the prosecution. Somewhat against expectation in the division, Dyett was found guilty and was given the mandatory sentence of being condemned to death, though the sentence was accompanied by a strong recommendation for mercy. However, the senior general to whom the case was referred, Sir Hubert Gough, Commander of the 5th Army, took a hard line, stating in his hand-written verdict (with heavy underlinings): 'I recommend that the sentence be carried out. If a private behaved as he did in such circumstances, it is highly probable that he would have been shot.' Thus in the time-honoured (or time-dishonoured) phrase Dyett was shot 'for the sake of example'. He was one of only three officers executed during the war.

In 1918 his case was taken up with some anger by Horatio Bottomley, the populist editor of the magazine *John Bull*, on the grounds that the trial and its outcome had been managed with scant regard for the normal demands of justice. It was claimed that Dyett had been led to expect that the worst that could befall him was the loss of his commission, and that he was not told of his death sentence until 7.45 p.m. on the night before he was executed, when an officer stepped into his room and read the warrant. 'We cannot bring back to life this young lad,' wrote Bottomley, 'who in our view was sacrificed, if not wantonly, then with a shocking disregard for just and humane methods. But we can insist that the whole system of Courts-Martial shall be drastically revised so that the soldier shall at least find as much protection in law as the civilian.' The result of *John Bull*'s campaign was that the case was raised in the House of Commons, though at a time of serious anxiety over the situation in France – the spring of 1918 saw a series of massive German attempts to snatch a victory before the unlimited forces of the United States could be brought to bear – it seems to have made few waves, or, in the words of the noted First World War historian John Terraine, to have generated 'more heat than light'.

But the case did go public, which fact, plus the consideration that Dyett was a member of his own division, suggests that Herbert was well versed in the ins and outs of this imbroglio when he wrote his novel. But Dyett had only recently joined the division, whereas in Herbert's story Harry Penrose, no natural soldier, serves through the long harrowing campaign in Gallipoli as well as in France, trying with desperate earnestness to make the grade, even volunteering to undertake one of the most challenging roles in trench warfare, that of a scout officer specialising in night patrols in No Man's Land. Thus Herbert's 'plot' covers a much larger span and produces a long, slow decline from high hopes and the best of intentions to ignominy and disgrace which can almost be seen as Shakespearean. Which is why Herbert's book is not the account of an unhappy mischance followed by an unfortunate outcome; it is, as its author calls it, a tragedy, exposing the fact that a military execution, while acceptable according to the then rules of war, could also be a grave error

in law. Hence the novel's telling first sentence: 'I am going to write down some of the
history of Harry Penrose, because I do not
think full justice has been done to him.'

However, an important caveat should be
entered here. It seems to me that ultimately
Herbert was less interested in the rights and
wrongs of executions than in the matter of
courage. It is as though he were anticipating the central thesis of that great classic
work, *The Anatomy of Courage*[2], by Lord
Moran, former First World War soldier and
medical adviser to many of the great and
famous, Churchill included, which was not
published until the last year of the Second
World War, 1945. Moran saw courage not
as an infinitely renewable resource, but as a
kind of bank balance, which it was all too
easy to expend. If you keep on paying out
the cheques, the time will come when there's
nothing left. You may be brave, but you can
also be broke. It's clear that Herbert saw
Harry Penrose in this light, as a man who
had poured out all his income in his efforts
to achieve the high standards he had set

[2] Moran, Lord, *The Anatomy of Courage* (London:
Constable, 1946)

himself and had arrived at the point where he was, effectively, bankrupt. Hence the tragic paradox that Harry was shot for cowardice, but, states Herbert's anonymous narrator with profound sincerity and conviction, 'he was one of the bravest men I ever knew'.

On the matter of executions, it should be noted that Herbert remained pointedly neutral. One senses his instincts were against them, but he left the subject open. Writes our narrator, doubtless echoing Herbert's own thoughts: 'I think I believe in the death penalty – I do not know. But I did not believe in Harry being shot.'

All this occurs on the novel's final page: there could hardly be a last page with more power to grip, disturb and shock. On that page Herbert throws down a gauntlet to his readers and leaves them to come to their own conclusions. It is like a speech to a jury; and we are the jury. The jury is still out.

But there is another matter to be aired, and here we enter into the realm of speculation. The death penalty for military crimes was abolished in 1929, after a sustained campaign in which the leading figure was a Labour Member of Parliament, Ernest Thurtle, who had served on the Western Front first in the ranks and later as an officer, and had been severely wounded during the Battle of Cambrai in late 1917. He had launched his campaign as far back as 1920 with a book entitled *Military Discipline and Democracy*, following this in 1924 with the publication of a pamphlet entitled *Shooting at Dawn: The Army Death Penalty at Work.* His purpose was to establish that the claim that executions during the war for cowardice and desertion had been miscarriages of justice and throughout the 1920s he used the annual debates on the Army Act to press his case. Finally, a number of senior soldiers rallied to his support and, despite a late challenge by the House of Lords, which he countered with an impassioned plea in the House of Commons, he won the day with a vote of 194 for his cause as opposed to 50 against. From 1929 onwards executions were legitimised only for capital offences that were capital charges in civil law.

Yet during the Second World War, at first even before the British Army was involved in serious fighting, powerful voices began to lobby for the ultimate sanction to be reinstated. By March 1940 the British

Commander-in-Chief in France, Lord Gort, was arguing that penal servitude was an insufficient deterrent for desertion, while subsequently in 1942, following serious setbacks in North Africa, the Commander-in-Chief, Middle East, Sir Claude Auchinleck, cabled the War Office requesting 'in strongest possible terms for the earliest possible agreement to reintroduce death penalty for specified offences', adding 'Recent desertions show alarming increase even amongst troops of highest category. Present punishments are insufficient.' The message behind these pleas was clear and simple: these two seasoned soldiers wanted the firing squad back.

In the end it was seen that, whatever the arguments from the field, the political dimension made reintroduction of the death penalty impossible. Legislation would be unavoidable and the mere fact of it would be counter-productive. As the authors of a recent major work on this subject, *Blindfold and Alone*[3], John Hughes-Wilson and

[3] Cornes, Catherine and Hughes-Wilson, John, *Blindfold and Alone: British Military Executions in the Great War* (London: Cassell, 2001)

Cathryn Corns, wrote: 'If the situation was really as bad as [was] claimed, advertising the army's problems would only make it worse and give Britain's enemies . . . a deeply damaging propaganda coup.'

Crucially the matter came to the desk of Winston Churchill, Prime Minister, Minister of Defence, and leader and galvaniser in chief of a nation fighting for its life. He said 'No' and there the buck stopped. Somehow one can't help feeling that Churchill's outright negative was more than a merely political gesture, it was a recognition that this was a practice long overdue for the historical dustbin. And I cannot but think that the seeds of this final, irreversible decision were sown when Churchill first read *The Secret Battle* many years earlier. In short, I venture to suggest that Herbert's novel effectively changed the course of legal and military history in this contentious area; it was, I believe, as important as that.

I hope the reader will forgive me if I conclude this Introduction with a personal coda.

I first visited the former Western Front in the autumn of 1975, when I went to France to research a television documentary I was making for the BBC on the subject of the Battle of the Somme. I took with me a number of keynote books, including Siegfried Sassoon's *Memoirs of an Infantry Officer*, *A Subaltern on the Somme* by Max Plowman, writing under the *nom de guerre* of Mark VII, and a paperback of Brian Gardner's iconic anthology of First World War poetry, *Up the Line to Death*[4].

Prowling the region of the Somme battlefield, late one afternoon I found myself at Beaucourt in the Ancre Valley, site of the Memorial to Herbert's 63rd (Royal Naval) Division. As has already been indicated, the village and its nearby station had been attacked by the division on 13 November 1916. This, however, was no routine run-of-the-mill action. Success was achieved over two days of extremely hard fighting at the horrific cost of almost 3,500 men killed, wounded and missing; which is clearly why this tiny Picardy village is home to the division's memorial, making Beaucourt, effectively, a kind of overseas capital.

[4] Gardner, Brian (ed.), *Up the Line to Death: The War Poets 1914–18* (London: Methuen & Co., 1964)

Subsequently most of the fallen of the attack were buried in a military cemetery nearby bearing the village's name. Prompted by the name I riffled through the pages of the Gardner anthology searching for a poem by someone I had thought to be an unlikely presence in so sombre a context: a poem by, of all people, A.P. Herbert. Alone in the cemetery I found myself walking through the lines of graves, reading the poem out loud and feeling profoundly moved: if at that time Herbert was, to me, mainly a humorist, here he was writing with the passion and emotion of the best-known war-poets.

Sometime in 1917, back in Beaucourt and visiting the cemetery in its temporary wartime condition, with the graves marked not by headstones but by wooden crosses, Herbert grieved for his fallen comrades, while, in poetic terms at least, resenting the presence of new arrivals in the regiment to whom the location had little or no meaning. There is a sense of raw immediacy in this poem, clearly suggesting that the events which prompted it were too recent, too painful, to produce any kind of mellow or nostalgic reflection. In homage to its author, and to help deepen understanding of this remarkable, multi-talented man, I take the liberty of quoting the poem in full. (It should be stated that the Dyett case was far from Herbert's mind when he wrote this poem; in the scheme of things it is ironic, but purely coincidental, that this very battle was to provide the source of his great war novel).

Beaucourt Revisited

I wandered up to Beaucourt; I took the river track,
And saw the lines we lived in before the Boche went back;
But Peace was now in Pottage, the front was far ahead,
The front had journeyed Eastward, and only left the dead.

And I thought, How long we lay there, and watched across the wire,
While the guns roared round the valley, and set the skies afire!
But now there are homes in Hamel and tents in the Vale of Hell,
And a camp at Suicide Corner, where half a regiment fell.

The new troops follow after, and tread the land
    we won,
To them 'tis so much hillside re-wrested from
    the Hun;
We only walk with reverence this sullen mile
    of mud;
The shell-holes hold our history, and half of
    them our blood.

Here, at the head at Peche Street, 'twas death
    to show your face;
To me it seemed like magic to linger in the
    place;
For me how many spirits hung round the
    Kentish Caves,
But the new men see no spirits – they only see
    the graves.

I found the half-dug ditches we fashioned for
    the fight
We lost a score of men there – young James
    was killed that night;
I saw the star-shells staring, I heard the bullets
    hail,
But the new troops pass unheeding – they
    never heard the tale.

I crossed the blood-red ribbon, that once was
    No Man's Land,
I saw a misty daybreak and a creeping minute-
    hand;
And here the lads went over, and there was
    Harmsworth shot,
And here was William lying – but the new
    men know them not.

And I said, 'There is still the river, and still
    the stiff, stark trees:
To treasure here our story, but there are only
    these;'
But under the white wood crosses the dead
    men answered low,
'The new men know not Beaucourt, but we
    are here – we know.'

Discovering and being moved by that poem meant that I was not surprised when, some years later, I came across *The Secret Battle* and recognised its unique quality. The republishing of that classic work in a fine new edition is the realisation of a long-held ambition.

THE
SECRET BATTLE

I

I AM going to write down some of the history
of Harry Penrose, because I do not think
full justice has been done to him, and because
there must be many other young men of his
kind who flung themselves into this war at the
beginning of it, and have gone out of it after
many sufferings with the unjust and ignorant
condemnation of their fellows. At times, it
may be, I shall seem to digress into the
dreary commonplaces of all war-chronicles,
but you will never understand the ruthless
progression of Penrose's tragedy without some
acquaintance with each chapter of his life in
the army.

He joined the battalion only a few days before
we left Plymouth for Gallipoli, a shy, intelligent-
looking person, with smooth, freckled skin and
quick, nervous movements ; and although he
was at once posted to my company we had not
become at all intimate when we steamed at last

into Mudros Bay. But he had interested me from the first, and at intervals in the busy routine of a troopship passing without escort through submarine waters I had been watching him and delighting in his keenness and happy disposition.

It was not my first voyage through the Mediterranean, though it was the first I had made in a transport, and I liked to see my own earlier enthusiasm vividly reproduced in him. Cape Spartel and the first glimpse of Africa ; Tangiers and Tarifa and all that magical hour's steaming through the narrow waters with the pink and white houses hiding under the hills ; Gibraltar Town shimmering and asleep in the noonday sun ; Malta and the bumboat women, carozzes swaying through the narrow, chattering streets ; cool drinks at cafés in a babel of strange tongues ; all these were to Penrose part of the authentic glamour of the East ; and he said so. I might have told him, with the fatuous pomp of wider experience, that they were in truth but a very distant reflection of the genuine East ; but I did not. For it was refreshing to see any one so frankly confessing to the sensations of adventure and romance. To other members of the officers' mess the spectacle of Gibraltar from the sea may have been more stimulating than the spectacle of Southend (though this is doubtful) ; but it is certain that few of them would have admitted the impeachment.

At Malta some of us spent an evening ashore, and sat for a little in a tawdry, riotous little café, where two poor singing women strove vainly to make themselves heard above the pandemonium of clinked glasses and bawled orders ; there we met many officers newly returned from the landing at Cape Helles, some of them with slight bodily wounds, but all of them with grievous injury staring out of their eyes. Those of them who would speak at all were voluble with anecdotes of horror and blood. Most of our own party had not yet lost the light-hearted mood in which men went to the war in those days ; the ' picnic ' illusion of war was not yet dispelled ; also, individually, no doubt, we had that curious confidence of the unblooded soldier that none of these strange, terrible things could ever actually happen to *us* ; we should for ever hang upon the pleasant fringes of war, sailing in strange seas, and drinking in strange towns, but never definitely entangled in the more crude and distasteful circumstances of battle. And if there were any of us with a secret consciousness that we deceived ourselves, to-night was no time to tear away the veil. Let there be lights and laughter and wine ; to-morrow, if need be, let us be told how the wounded had drowned in the wired

shallows, and reckon the toll of that unforget-
table exploit and the terrors that were still at
work.   And so we would not be dragooned into
seriousness by these messengers from the
Peninsula ; but rather, with no injury to their
feelings, laughed at their croakings and continued to drink.

But Harry Penrose was different. He was
all eagerness to hear every detail, hideous and
heroic.

There was one officer present, from the
29th Division, a man about forty, with a
tanned, melancholy face and great solemn eyes,
which, for all the horrors he related, seemed to
have something yet more horrible hidden in
their depths.   Him Harry plied with questions,
his reveller's mood flung impatiently aside ;
and the man seemed ready to tell him things,
though from his occasional reservations and
sorrowful smile I knew that he was pitying Harry
for his youth, his eagerness, and his ignorance.

Around us were the curses of overworked
waiters, and the babble of loud conversations,
and the smell of spilt beer ; there were two
officers uproariously drunk, and in the distance
pathetic snatches of songs were heard from the
struggling singer on the dais. We were in one
of the first outposts of the Empire, and halfway
to one of her greatest adventures. And this
excited youth at my side was the only one of all

that throng who was ready to hear the truth of it, and to speak of death. I lay emphasis on this incident, because it well illustrates his attitude towards the war at that time (which too many have now forgotten), and because I then first found the image which alone reflects the many curiosities of his personality.

He was like an imaginative, inquisitive child ; a child that cherishes a secret gallery of pictures in its mind, and must continually be feeding this storehouse with new pictures of the unknown ; that is not content with a vague outline of something that is to come, a dentist, or a visit, or a doll, but will not rest till the experience is safely put away in its place, a clear, uncompromising picture, to be taken down and played with at will.

Moreover, he had the fearlessness of a child —but I shall come to that later.

And so we came to Mudros, threading a placid way between the deceitful Aegean Islands. Harry loved them because they wore so green and inviting an aspect, and again I did not undeceive him and tell him how parched and austere, how barren of comfortable grass and shade he would find them on closer acquaintance. We steamed into Mudros Bay at the end of an unbelievable sunset ; in the great harbour were gathered regiments of ships— battleship, cruiser, tramp, transport, and trawler, and as the sun sank into the western hills, the masts and the rigging of all of them were radiant with its last rays, while all their decks and hulls lay already in the soft blue dusk. There is something extraordinarily soothing in the almost imperceptible motion of a big steamer gliding at slow speed to her anchorage ; as I leaned over the rail of the boat-deck and heard the tiny bugle-calls float across from the French or English warships, and watched the miniature crews at work upon their decks, I became aware that Penrose was similarly engaged close at hand, and it seemed to me an opportunity to learn something of the history of this strange young man.

Beginning with his delight in the voyage and all the marvellous romance of our surroundings, I led him on to speak of himself. Both his parents had died when he was a boy at school. They had left him enough to go to Oxford upon (without the help of the Exhibition he had won), and he had but just completed his second year there when the war broke out. For some mysterious reason he had immediately enlisted instead of applying for a commission, like his friends. I gathered—though not from any-thing he directly said—that he had had a hard time in the ranks. The majority of his companions in training had come down from the north with the first draft of Tynesiders ; and though, God knows, the Tynesider as a fighting man has been unsurpassed in this war, they were a wild, rough crowd before they became soldiers, and I can understand that for a high-strung, sensitive boy of his type the intimate daily round of eating, talking, and sleeping with them, must have made large demands on his patriotism and grit. But he said it did him good ; and it was only the pestering of his guardian and relations that after six months forced him to take a commission. He had a curious lack of confidence in his fitness to be an officer—a feeling which is deplorably absent in hundreds not half as fit as he was ; but from what I had seen of his handling of his platoon on the voyage (and the men are difficult after a week or two at sea) I was able to assure him that he need have no qualms. He was, I discovered, pathetically full of military ambitions ; he dreamed already, he confessed, of decorations and promotions and glorious charges. In short, he was like many another undergraduate officer of those days in his eagerness and readiness for sacrifice, but far removed from the common type in his roman-tic, imaginative outlook towards the war. ' Romantic ' is the only word, I think, and it is melancholy for me to remember that even then I said to myself, ' I wonder how long the romance will last, my son.'

But I could not guess just how terrible was to be its decay.

II

We were not to be long at Mudros. For three days we lay in the sweltering heat of the great hill-circled bay, watching the warships come and go, and buying fruit from the little Greek sailing boats which fluttered round the harbour. These were days of hot anxiety about one's kit; hourly each officer reorganized and redisposed his exiguous belongings, and re-weighed his valise, and jettisoned yet more precious articles of comfort, lest the weight regulations be violated and for the sake of an extra shirt the whole of one's equipment be cast into the sea by the mysterious figure we believed to watch over these things. Afterwards we found that all our care was in vain, and in the comfortless camps of the Peninsula bitterly bewailed the little luxuries we had needlessly left behind, there so unattainable. Down in the odorous troop-decks the men wrote long letters describing the battles in which they were already engaged, and the sound of mythical guns.

But on the third day came our sailing orders. In the evening a little trawler, promoted to the dignity of a fleet-sweeper, came alongside, and all the regiment of gross, overloaded figures, festooned with armament and bags of food, and strange, knobbly parcels, tumbled heavily over the side. Many men have written of the sailing of the first argosy of troopships from that bay ; and by this time the spectacle of departing troops was an old one to the vessels there. But this did not diminish the quality of their farewells. The rails of the King's ships were thick with men as we passed, and they sent us a great wave of cheering that filled the heart with sadness and resolution.

In one of the French ships was a party of her crew high up somewhere above the deck, and they sang for us with surprising precision and feeling the ' Chant du Départ ' ; so moving was this that even the stolid Northerners in our sweeper were stirred to make some more articulate acknowledgment than the official British cheer ; and one old pitman, searching among his memories of some Lancashire music-hall, dug out a rough version of the ' Marseillaise.' By degrees all our men took up the tune and sang it mightily, with no suspicion of words ; and the officers, not less timidly, joined in, and were proud of the men for what they had done. For many were moved in that moment who were never moved before. But while we were yet warm with cheering and the sense of knighthood, we cleared the boom and shivered a little in the breeze of the open sea.

The sun went down, and soon it was very cold in the sweeper : and in each man's heart I think there was a chill. There were no more songs, but the men whispered in small groups, or stood silent, shifting uneasily their wearisome packs. For now we were indeed cut off from civilization and committed to the unknown. The transport we had left seemed a very haven of comfort and security ; one thought longingly of white tables in the saloon, and the unfriendly linen bags of bully-beef and biscuits we carried were concrete evidence of a new life. The war seemed no longer remote, and each of us realized indignantly that we were personally involved in it. So for a little all these soldiers had a period of serious thought unusual in the soldier's life. But as we neared the Peninsula the excitement and novelty and the prospect of exercising cramped limbs brought back valour and cheerfulness.

At Malta we had heard many tales of the still terrifying ordeal of landing under fire. But such terrors were not for us. There was a bright moon, and, as we saw the pale cliffs of Cape Helles, all, I think, expected each moment a torrent of shells from some obscure quarter. But instead an unearthly stillness brooded over the two bays, and only a Morse lamp blinking at the sweeper suggested that any living thing was there. There came over the water a strange musty smell ; some said it was the smell of the dead, and some the smell of an incinerator ; myself I do not know, but it was the smell of the Peninsula for ever, which no man can forget. We disembarked at a pier of rafts by the *River Clyde*, and stumbled eagerly ashore. And now we were in the very heart of heroic things. Nowhere, I think, was the new soldier plunged so suddenly into the genuine scenes of war as he was at Gallipoli ; in France there was a long transition of training-camps and railway trains and billets, and he moved by easy gradations to the firing-line. But here, a few hours after a night in linen sheets, we stood suddenly on the very sand where, but three weeks before, those hideous machine-guns on the cliffs had mown down that immortal party of April 25. And in that silver stillness it was difficult to believe.

We shambled off up the steady slope between two cliffs, marvelling that any men could have prevailed against so perfect a ' field of fire '. By now we were very tired, and it was heavy work labouring through the soft sand. Queer, Moorish-looking figures in white robes peered at us from dark corners, and here and there a man poked a tousled head from a hole in the ground, and blinked upon our progress. Some

one remarked that it reminded him of nothing
so much as the native camp at Earl's Court on
a fine August evening, and that indeed was the
effect.

After a little the stillness was broken by a
sound which we could not conceal from ourselves was 'the distant rattle of musketry';
somewhere a gun fired startlingly; and now as
we went each man felt vaguely that at any
minute we might be plunged into the thick of
a battle, laden as we were, and I think each
man braced himself for a desperate struggle.
Such is the effect of marching in the dark to an
unknown destination. Soon we were halted in
a piece of apparently waste land circled by
trees, and ordered to dig ourselves a habitation
at once, for 'in the morning' it was whispered
'the Turks search all this ground.' Everything was said in hoarse, mysterious whispers,
presumably to conceal our observations from
the ears of the Turks five miles away. But
then we did not know they were five miles
away; we had no idea where they were
or where we were ourselves. Men glanced
furtively at the North Star for guidance, and
were pained to find that, contrary to their
military teaching, it told them nothing. Even
the digging was carried on a little stealthily till
it was discovered that the Turks were not
behind those trees. The digging was a comfort

to the men, who, being pitmen, were now in their element ; and the officers found solace in whispering to each other that magical communication about the expected ' searching ' ; it was the first technical word they had used ' in the field,' and they were secretly proud to know what it meant.

In a little the dawn began, and the grey trees took shape ; the sun came up out of Asia, and we saw at last the little sugarloaf peak of Achi Baba, absurdly pink and diminutive in the distance. A man's first frontal impression of that great rampart, with the outlying slopes masking the summit, was that it was disappointingly small ; but when he had lived under and upon it for a while, day by day, it seemed to grow in menace and in bulk, and ultimately became an overpowering monster, pervading all his life ; so that it worked upon men's nerves, and almost everywhere in the Peninsula they were painfully conscious that every movement they made could be watched from somewhere on that massive hill.

But now the kitchens had come, and there was breakfast and viscous, milkless tea. We discovered that all around our seeming solitude the earth had been peopled with sleepers, who now emerged from their holes ; there was a stir of washing and cooking and singing, and the smoke went up from the wood fires in the clear, cool air. D Company officers made their camp under an olive-tree, with a view over the blue water to Samothrace and Imbros, and now in the early cool, before the sun had gathered his noonday malignity, it was very pleasant. At seven o'clock the ' searching ' began. A mile away, on the northern cliffs, the first shell burst, stampeding a number of horses. The long-drawn warning scream and the final crash gave all the expectant battalion a faintly pleasurable thrill, and as each shell came a little nearer the sensation remained. No one was afraid ; without the knowledge of experience no one could be seriously afraid on this cool, sunny morning in the grove of olive-trees. Those chill hours in the sweeper had been much more alarming. The common sensation was : ' At last I am really under fire ; to-day I shall write home and tell them about it.' And then, when it seemed that the line on which the shells were falling must, if continued, pass through the middle of our camp, the firing mysteriously ceased.

Harry, I know, was disappointed ; personally, I was pleased.

· · · · ·

I learned more about Harry that afternoon. He had been much exhausted by the long night, but was now refreshed and filled with an almost childish enthusiasm by the pictorial attractions of the place. For this enthusiastic soul one thing only was lacking in the site of the camp : the rise of the hill, which here runs down the centre of the Peninsula, hid from us the Dardanelles. These, he said, must immediately be viewed. It was a bright afternoon of blue skies and gentle air—not yet had the dry north-east wind come to plague us with dust-clouds— and all the vivid colours of the scene were unspoiled. We walked over the hill through the parched scrub, where lizards darted from under our feet and tortoises lay comatose in the scanty shade, and came to a kind of inland cliff, where the Turks had had many riflemen at the landing, for all the ground was littered with empty cartridges. And there was unfolded surely the most gorgeous panorama this war has provided for prosaic Englishmen to see. Below was a cool, inviting grove of imperial cypresses ; all along the narrow strip between us and the shore lay the rest-lines of the French, where moved lazy figures in blue and red, and black Senegalese in many colours. To the left was the wide sweep of Morto Bay, and beyond the first section of Achi Baba rising to De Tott's Battery in terraces of olives and vines. But what caught the immediate eye, what we had come to see and had sailed hither to fight for, was that strip of marvellously blue water before us, deep, generous blue, like a Chinese bowl. On the farther shore, towards the entrance to the Straits, we could see a wide green plain, and beyond and to the left, peak after peak of the mountains of Asia ; and far away in the middle distance there was a glint of snow from some regal summit of the Anatolian Mountains.

That wide green plain was the Plain of Troy. The scarcity of classical scholars in Expeditionary Forces, and the wearisome observations of pressmen on the subject of Troy, have combined to belittle the significance of the classical surroundings of the Gallipoli campaign. I myself am a stolid, ill-read person, but I confess that the spectacle of those historic flats was not one, in diplomatic phrase, which I could view with indifference. On Harry, ridiculously excited already, the effect was almost alarming. He became quite lyrical over two little sweepers apparently anchored near the mouth of the Straits. ' That,' he said, ' must have been where the Greek fleet lay. God ! it 's wonderful.' Up on the slope towards De Tott's Battery the guns were busy, and now and then Asiatic Annie sent over a large shell from the region of Achilles' tomb, which burst ponderously in the sea off Cape Helles. And there we sat on the stony edge of the cliff and

talked of Achilles and Hector and Diomed and
Patroclus and the far-sounding bolts of Jove.
I do not defend or exalt this action ; but this
is a truthful record of a man's personality,
and I simply state what occurred. And I
confess that with the best wish in the world
I was myself becoming a little bored with Troy,
when in the middle of a sentence he suddenly
became silent and gazed across the Straits
with a fixed, pinched look in his face, like a
man who is reminded of some far-off calamity
he had forgotten. For perhaps a minute he
maintained this rigid aspect, and then as
suddenly relaxed, murmuring in a tone of
inflexible determination, ' I will.' It was not
in me not to inquire into the nature of this
passionate intention, and somehow I induced
him to explain.

It seemed that in spite of his genuine
academic successes and a moderate popularity
at school and at Oxford he had suffered from
early boyhood from a curious distrust of his
own capacity in the face of anything he had to
do. In a measure, no doubt, this had even
contributed to his successes. For his nervousness took the form of an intimate, silent brooding
over any ordeal that lay before him, whether it
was a visit to his uncle, or ' Schools,' or a
dance : he would lie awake for hours imagining
all conceivable forms of error and failure and

humiliation that might befall him in his endeavour. And though he was to this extent forewarned and forearmed, it must have been a painful process. And it explained to me the puzzling intervals of melancholy which I had seen darkening his usually cheerful demeanour.

'You remember last night,' he said, ' I had been detailed to look after the baggage when we disembarked, and take charge of the unloading party ? As far as I know I did the job all right, except for losing old Tompkins' valise— but you can't think how much worry and anxiety it gave me *beforehand*. All the time on the sweeper I was imagining the hundreds of possible disasters : the working-party not turning up, and me left alone on the boat with the baggage—the Colonel's things being dropped overboard—a row with the M.L.O.—getting the baggage ashore, and then losing the battalion, or the working-party, or the baggage. It all worked out quite simply, but I tell you, Benson, it gave me hell. And it 's always the same. That 's really why I didn't take a commission— because I couldn't imagine myself drilling men once without becoming a permanent laughing-stock. I know now that I was a fool about that—I usually do find that out—but I can't escape the feeling next time.

' And now, it 's not only little things like that, but that 's what I feel about the whole war. I 've a terror of being a failure in it, a failure out here—you know, a sort of regimental dud. I 've heard of lots of them ; the kind of man that nobody gives an important job because he 's sure to muck it up (though I do believe Eccleston 's more likely to be that than me). But that 's what I was thinking just now. Somehow, looking at this view—Troy and all that—and thinking how those Greeks sweated blood for ten years on afternoons like this, doing their duty for the damned old kings, and how we 've come out here to fight in the same place thousands of years afterwards, and we still know about them and remember their names—well, it gave me a kind of inspiration ; I don't know why. I 've got a bit of confidence —God knows how long it will last—but I swear I won't be a failure, I won't be the battalion dud—and I 'll have a damned good try to get a medal of some sort and be like—like Achilles or somebody.'

Sheer breathlessness put a sudden end to this outburst, and since it was followed by a certain shyness at his own revelations I did not probe deeper. But I thought to myself that this young man's spirit of romance would die hard ; I did not know whether it would ever die ; for certainly I had never seen that spirit working so powerfully in any man as a living incentive to achievement. And I tell you all this, because I want you to understand how it was with him in the beginning.

But now the bay was in shadow below us ; on the hill the solemn stillness that comes over all trenches in the hour before dusk had already descended, and away towards the cape the Indians were coming out to kneel in prayer beside the alien sea.

The Romance of War was in full song. And, scrambling down the cliff, we bathed almost reverently in the Hellespont.

THOSE first three days were for many of us, who did not know the mild autumn months, the most pleasant we spent on the Peninsula. The last weeks of May had something of the quality of an old English summer, and the seven plagues of the Peninsula had not yet attained the intolerable violence of June and July. True, the inhabited portion of the narrow land we had won already was a wilderness ; the myrtle, and rock-rose, and tangled cistus, and all that wealth of spring flowers in which the landing parties had fallen and died in April, had long been trodden to death, and there were wide stretches of yellow desert where not even the parched scrub survived. But in the two and a half miles of bare country which lay between the capes and the foot-hills of Achi Baba was one considerable oasis of olives and stunted oaks, and therein, on the slopes of the ridge, was our camp fortunately set. The word ' camp ' contains an unmerited compliment to the place. The manner of its birth was characteristic of military arrangements in those days. When we were told, on that first mysterious midnight, to dig ourselves a shelter against the morning's

'searching,' we were far from imagining that
what we dug would be our Peninsular ' home '
and haven of rest from the firing-line for many
months to come. And so we made what we
conceived to be the quickest and simplest form
of shelter against a merely temporary danger—
long, straight, untraversed ditches, running
parallel to and with but a few yards between
each other. No worse form of permanent
dwelling-place could conceivably have been
constructed, for the men were cramped in these
places with a minimum of comfort and a
maximum of danger. No man could climb
out of his narrow drain without casting a shower
of dust from the crumbling parapet on to his
sleeping neighbour in the next ditch; and
three large German shells could have destroyed
half the regiment. Yet there were many such
camps, most of them lacking the grateful
concealment of our trees. Such targets even
the Turkish artillery must sometimes hit.
There were no dug-outs in the accepted sense
of the Western Front, no deep, elaborate,
stair-cased chambers, hollowed out by miners
with miners' material. *Our* dug-outs *were*
dug-outs in truth, shallow excavations scooped
in the surface of the earth. The only roof for
a man against sun and shells was a waterproof
sheet stretched precariously over his hole.
It is sufficient testimony to the poverty of the

Turkish artillery that with such naked concen-
trations of men scattered about the Peninsula,
casualties in the rest-camps were so few.

Each officer had his own private hole, set
democratically among the men's; and an
officers' mess was simply made by digging a
larger hole, and roofing it with *two* waterproof
sheets instead of one. There was no luxury
among the infantry there, and the gulf which
yawned between the lives of officer and man
in France in the way of material comfort was
barely discernible in Gallipoli. Food was dull
and monotonous : for weeks we had only
bully-beef and biscuits, and a little coarse
bacon and tea, but it was the same for all, one
honourable equality of discomfort. At first
there were no canteen supplies, and when
some newcomer came from one of the islands
with a bottle of champagne and another of
chartreuse, we drank them with ' bully ' and
cast-iron biscuit. Drinking water was as
precious as the elixir of life, and almost as un-
obtainable, but officer and man had the same
ration to eke out through the thirsty day.
Wells were sunk, and sometimes immediately
condemned, and when we knew the water was
clear and sweet to taste, it was hard to have it
corrupted with the metallic flavour of chemicals
by the medical staff. Then indeed did a man
learn to love water ; then did he learn discipline,

when he filled his water-bottle in the morning
with the exiguous ration of the day, and fought
with the desperate craving to put it to his lips
and there and then gurgle down his fill.

In the spring nights it was very cold, and
men shivered in their single blanket under the
unimaginable stars ; but very early the sun
came up, and by five o'clock all the camp were
singing ; and there were three hours of fresh
coolness when it was very good to wash in a
canvas bucket, and smoke in the sun before
the torrid time came on ; and again at seven,
when the sun sat perched on the great rock of
Samothrace, and Imbros was set in a fleecy bed
of pink and saffron clouds, there were two hours
of pure physical content ; but these, I think,
were more nearly perfect than the morning
because they succeeded the irritable fevers of the
day. Then the crickets in the branches sang
less tediously, and the flies melted away, and
all over the Peninsula the wood fires began to
twinkle in the dusk, as the men cooked over
a few sticks the little delicacies which were
preserved for this hour of respite. When we
had done we sat under our olive-tree in the
clear twilight, and watched the last aeroplanes
sail home to Rabbit Islands, and talked and
argued till the glow-worms glimmering in the
scrub, and up the hill the long roll of the
Turks' rapid fire, told us that darkness was at

hand, and the chill dew sent us into our crannies to sleep.

So we were not sorry for three days of quiet in the camp before we went up the hill ; Harry alone was all eagerness to reach the firing-line with the least possible delay. But then Harry was like none of us ; indeed, none of us were like each other. It would have been strange if we had been. War-chroniclers have noted with an accent of astonishment the strange diversity of persons to be found in units of the New Army, and the essential sameness of their attitude to the war. As if a man were to go into the Haymarket and be surprised if the first twelve pedestrians there were not of the same profession ; were then to summon them to the assistance of a woman in the hands of a rough, and be still surprised at the similarity of their methods.

We were, in truth, a motley crowd, gathered from everywhere ; but when we sat under that olive-tree we were very much alike—with the single exception of Harry.

Egerton, our company commander, a man of about thirty, with a round face, and a large head, was a stockbroker by profession, and, rather improbably, an old Territorial by pastime. He was an excellent company commander, but would have made a still more admirable second-in-command, for his training in figures and his meticulous habits in such things as the keeping of accounts were just what are required of a second-in-command and were lamentably deficient in myself. The intricacies of Acquittance Rolls and Imprest Accounts, and page 3 of the Soldier's Pay-Book, were meat and drink to him, and in general I must confess that I shamefully surrendered such dainties to him.

Harry Penrose had the 14th Platoon. Of the other three subalterns perhaps the most interesting was Hewett. He, like Harry, had been at Oxford before the war, though they had never come together there. He was a fair, dreamy person, of remarkably good looks. Alone of all the ' young Apollos ' I have known did he at all deserve that title. Most of these have been men of surpassing stupidity and material tastes, but Hewett added to his physical qualifications something of the mental fineness which presumably one should expect of even a modern Apollo. Intensely fastidious, he frankly detested the war, and all the dirt and disgust he must personally encounter. Like Harry, he was an idealist—but more so ; for he could not idealize the war. But the shrinking of his spirit had no effect on his conduct : he was no less courageous than Harry or any one else, and no less keen to see the thing through. Only, at that time, he was

a little less blind. A year senior to Harry, he
had taken Greats in 1914, and though his
degree had been disappointingly low he had not
yet lost the passionate attachment of the
' Greats ' man to philosophy and thoughts of
the Ultimate Truths. Sometimes he would
try to induce one of us to talk with him of his
religious and philosophical doubts ; but in
that feverish place it was too difficult for us,
and usually he brooded over his problems
alone.

Eustace, of the 16th Platoon, was a journalist
by repute, though it was never discovered to
what journal, if any, he was specially attached.
His character was more attractive than his
appearance, which was long, awkward, and
angular ; and if he had ever been to school, he
would have been quite undeservedly unpopular
for not playing games : undeservedly—because
one could not conceive of him as playing any
game. Physically, indeed, he was one of
Nature's gawks ; intellectually he was nimble,
not to say athletic, with an acute and deeply
logical mind. As a companion, more especially
a companion in war, he was made sometimes
tedious by a habit of cynicism and a passion
for argument. The cynicism, I think, had
developed originally from some early grievance
against Society, had been adopted as an effective
pose, and had now become part of his nature.

Whatever its origin it was wearing to us, for
in the actual scenes of war one likes to cling to
one's illusions while any shred of them remains,
and would rather they faded honourably under
the gentle influence of time than be torn to
fragments in a moment by reasoned mockery.
But Eustace was never tired of exhibiting the
frailty and subterfuge of all men, particularly
in their relations to the war; the *Nation*
arrived for him as regularly as the German
submarines would allow, and all his views were
in that sense distinctly 'National.'   If any
of us were rash enough to read that paper ourselves, we were inevitably provoked to some
comment which led to a hot wrangle on the
Public Schools, or Kitchener, or the rights of
the war, and the pleasant calm of the dusk was
marred.   For Eustace could always meet us
with a powerfully logical case, and while in
spirit we revolted against his heresies, we were
distressed by the appeal they made to our
reluctant reasons.   Harry, the most ingenuous
of us all and the most devoted to his illusions,
was particularly worried by this conflict.   It
seemed very wrong to him that a man so loyal
and gallant in his personal relations with others
should trample so ruthlessly on their dearest
opinions.

Burnett was of a very different type.   Tall
and muscular, with reddish hair and vivid blue

eyes, he looked (as he wanted to look) a ' man of action ' by nature and practice. He had ' knocked about ' for some years in Africa and Australia (a process which had failed equally to establish his fortunes or soften his rough edges), and from the first he affected the patronizing attitude of the experienced campaigner. The little discomforts of camp life were nothing to him, for were they not part of his normal life ? And when I emerged from my dug-out pursued, as I thought, by a ferocious centipede, he held forth for a long time on the best method of dispatching rattlesnakes in the Umgoga, or some such locality. By degrees, however, as life became more unbearable, the conviction dawned upon us that he was no less sensible to heat and hunger and thirst than mere ' temporary ' campaigners, and rather more ready to utter his complaints. Finally, the weight of evidence became overwhelming, and it was whispered at the end of our first week at Gallipoli that ' Burnett was bogus '. The quality of being ' bogus ' was in those days the last word in military condemnation ; and in Burnett's case events showed the verdict to be lamentably correct.

So we were a strangely assorted crowd, only alike, as I have said, in that we were keen on the winning of this war and resolved to do our personal best towards that end. Of the five of us, Hewett and Eustace had the most influence on Harry. Me he regarded as a solid kind of wall that would never let him down, or be guilty of any startling deviations from the normal. By Hewett he was personally and spiritually attracted ; by Eustace alternately fascinated and disturbed. And it was a very bad day for Harry when Hewett's death removed that gentle, comfortable influence.

II

We were ordered to relieve the ——'s at midnight on the fourth day, and once again we braced ourselves for the last desperate battle of our lives. All soldiers go through this process during their first weeks of active service every time they ' move ' anywhere. Immense expectations, vows, fears, prayers, fill their minds ; and nothing particular happens. Only the really experienced soldier knows that it is the exception and not the rule for anything particular to happen ; and the heroes of romance and history who do not move a muscle when told that they are to attack at dawn are generally quite undeserving of praise, since long experience has taught them that the attack is many times more likely to be cancelled than to occur. Until it actually does happen they will not believe in it ; they make all proper preparations, but quite rightly do not move a muscle. We, however, were now to have our first illustration of this great military truth. For, indeed, we were to have no battle. Yet that night's march to the trenches was an experience that made full compensation. It was already dusk when we moved out of the rest-camp, and the moon was not up. As usual in new units, the leading platoons went off at a reckless canter, and stumbling after them in the gathering shadows over rocky, precipitous slopes, and in and out of the clumps of bush, falling in dark holes on to indignant sleepers, or maddeningly entangled in hidden strands of wire, the rear companies were speedily out of touch. To a heavily laden infantryman there are few things more exasperating than a night march into the line conducted too fast. If the country be broken and strewn with obstacles, at which each man must wait while another climbs or drops or wrestles or wades in front of him, and must then laboriously scamper after him in the shadows lest he, and thereby all those behind him, be lost ; if the country be unknown to him, so that, apart from purely military considerations, the fear of being lost is no small thing, for a man knows that he may wander all night alone in the dark, surrounded by unknown dangers, cut off from sleep, and rations, and the friendly voices of companions,

a jest among them when he discovers them :
then such a march becomes a nightmare.

On this night it dawned gradually on those
in front that they were unaccompanied save by
the 1st platoon, and a long halt, and much
shouting and searching, gathered most of the
regiment together, hot, cursing, and already
exhausted. And now we passed the five white
Water Towers, standing mysteriously in a
swamp, and came out of the open country into
the beginning of a gully. These ' gullies ' were
deep, steep-sided ravines, driven through all the
lower slopes of Achi Baba, and carrying in the
spring a thin stream of water, peopled by many
frogs, down to the Straits or the sea. It was
easier going here, for there was a rough track
beside the stream to follow ; yet, though those
in front were marching, as they thought, with
unnecessary deliberation, the rear men of each
platoon were doubling round the corners among
the trees, and cursing as they ran. There was
then a wild hail of bullets in all those gullies,
since for many hours of each night the Turk
kept up a sustained and terrible rapid fire from
his trenches far up the hill, and, whether by
design or bad shooting, the majority of these
bullets passed high over our trenches, and fell
hissing in the gully-bed.

So now all the air seemed full of the humming,
whistling things, and all round in the gully-banks

and the bushes by the stream there were vicious spurts as they fell. It was always a marvel how few casualties were caused by this stray fire, and to-night we were chiefly impressed with this wonder. In the stream the frogs croaked incessantly with a note of weary indifference to the medley of competing noises. At one point there was a kind of pot-hole in the stream where the water squeezing through made a kind of high-toned wail, delivered with stabbing emphasis at regular intervals. So weird was this sound, which could be heard many hundred yards away and gradually asserted itself above all other contributions to that terrible din, that many of the men, already mystified and excited, said to themselves that this was the noise of the explosive bullets of which they had heard.

Soon we were compelled to climb out of the gully-path to make way for some descending troops, and stumbled forward with a curious feeling of nakedness high up in open ground. Here the bullets were many times multiplied, and many of us said that we could feel them passing between us. Indeed, one or two men were hit, but though we did not know it most of these near-sounding bullets flew high above us. After a little we were halted, and lay down, wondering, in the sibilant dark ; then we moved on and halted again, and realized suddenly that we were very tired. At the head of the column the guide had lost his way, and could not find the entrance to the communication trench ; and here in the most exposed area of all that Peninsula we must wait until he did. The march was an avoidable piece of mismanagement ; the whole regiment was being unnecessarily endangered. But none of this we knew ; so very few men were afraid. We were still in the bliss of ignorance. It seemed to us that these strange proceedings must be a part of the everyday life of the soldier. If they were not, we raw creatures should not have been asked to endure them. We had no standard of safety or danger by which to estimate our position ; and so the miraculous immunity we were enjoying was taken as a matter of course, and we were blissfully unafraid. At the same time we were extremely bored and tired, and the sweat cooled on us in the chill night air. And when at last we came into the deep communication trench we felt that the end of this weariness must surely be near. But the worst exasperations of relieving an unknown line were still before us. It was a two-mile trudge in the narrow ditches to the front line. No war correspondent has ever described such a march ; it is not included in the official ' horrors of war ' ; but this is the kind of thing which, more than battle and blood, harasses the spirit

of the infantryman, and composes his life.
The communication trenches that night were
good and deep and dry, and free from the
awfulness of mud; but they were very few,
and unintelligently used. There had been an
attack that day, and coming by the same trench
was a long stream of stretchers and wounded
men, and odd parties coming to fetch water
from the well, and whole battalions relieved
from other parts of the line. Our men had
been sent up insanely with full packs; for
a man so equipped to pass another naked
in the narrow ditch would have been difficult;
when all those that he meets have also straps
and hooks and excrescences about them,
each separate encounter means heart-break-
ing entanglements and squeezes and sudden
paroxysms of rage. That night we stood a
total of hours hopelessly jammed in the suffocating trench, with other troops trying to get
down. A man stood in those crushes, unable to
sit down, unable to lean comfortably against
the wall because of his pack, unable even to get
his hand to his water-bottle and quench his
intolerable thirst, unable almost to breathe for
the hot smell of herded humanity. Only a thin
ribbon of stars overhead, remotely roofing his
prison, reminded him that indeed he was still
in the living world and not pursuing some
hideous nightmare. At long last some one

would take charge of the situation, and by
sheer muscular fighting for space the two masses
would be extricated. Then we moved on
again. And now each man has become a mere
lifeless automaton. Every few yards there is a
wire hanging across the trench at the height of
a man's eyes, and he runs blindly into it, or it
catches in the piling-swivel of his rifle ; painfully he removes it, or in a fit of fury tears the
wire away with him. Or there is a man lying
in a corner with a wounded leg crying out to
each passer-by not to tread on him, or a stretcher
party slowly struggling against the tide.
Mechanically each man grapples with these
obstacles, mechanically repeats the ceaseless
messages that are passed up and down, and
the warning ' Wire,' ' Stretcher party,' ' Step
up,' to those behind, and stumbles on. He is
only conscious of the dead weight of his load,
and the braces of his pack biting into his
shoulders, of his thirst, and the sweat of his
body, and the longing to lie down and sleep.
When we halt men fall into a doze as they stand
and curse pitifully when they are urged on
from behind.

We reach the inhabited part of the line, and
the obstacles become more frequent, for there
are traverses every ten yards and men sleeping
on the floor, and a litter of rifles, water-cans,
and scattered equipment. For ever we wind

round the endless traverses, and squeeze past
the endless host we are relieving ; and sometimes the parapet is low or broken or thin, or
there is a dangerous gap, and we are told to
keep our heads down, and dully pass back the
message so that it reaches men meaninglessly
when they have passed the danger-point, or are
still far from it. All the time there is a wild
rattle of rapid fire from the Turks, and bullets
hammer irritably on the parapet, or fly singing
overhead. When a man reached his destined
part of the trench that night there were still
long minutes of exasperation before him ; for
we were inexperienced troops, and first of all
the men crowded in too far together, and must
turn about, and press back so as to cover the
whole ground to be garrisoned ; then they
would flock like sad sheep too far in the opposite
direction. This was the subaltern's bad time ;
for the officer must squeeze backwards and
forwards, struggling to dispose properly his
own sullen platoon, and it was hard for him to
be patient with their stupidity, for, like them,
he only longed to fling off his cursed equipment
and lie down and sleep for ever. He, like
them, had but one thought, that if there were
to be no release from the hateful burden that
clung to his back, and cut into his shoulders
and ceaselessly impeded him, if there were to
be no relief for his thirst and the urgent aching

of all his body—he must soon sink down
and curse like a fool.

III

Harry's platoon was settled in when I
found him, hidden away somewhere in the
third (Reserve) line. He had conscientiously
posted a few sentries, and done all those things
which a good platoon commander should do,
and was lying himself in a sort of stupor of
fatigue. Physically he was not strong, rather
frail, in fact, for the infantry; he had a narrow
chest and slightly round shoulders, and his
heart would not have passed a civilian doctor;
and—from my own experience—I knew that
the march must have tried him terribly. But
a little rest had soothed the intense nervous
irritation whose origins I have tried to describe,
and his spirit was as sturdy as ever. He
struggled to his feet and leaned over the
parados with me. The moon was now high
up in the north-east; the Turks had ceased
their rapid fire at moonrise, and now an
immense peace wrapped the Peninsula. We
were high up on the centre slopes of Achi
Baba, and all the six miles which other men
had conquered lay bathed in moonlight below
us. Far away at the cape we could see the
long, green lights of the hospital ships, and all

about us were glow-worms in the scrub. Left and right the pale parapets of trenches crept like dim-seen snakes into the little valleys, and vanished over the opposite slopes. Only a cruiser off-shore firing lazily at long intervals disturbed the slumberous stillness. No better sedative could have been desired.

' How did you like the march ? ' I said.

' Oh, all right ; one of my men was wounded, I believe, but I didn't see him.'

' All right ? ' I said. ' Personally I thought it was damned awful ; it 's a marvel that any of us are here at all. I hear A Company 's still adrift, as it is.'

' Well, anyhow *we* got here,' said Harry. ' Wonderful spot this. Look at those glow-worms.'

I was anxious to know what impression the night had made on Harry, but these and other answers gave me no real clue. I had a suspicion that it had, in truth, considerably distressed him, but any such effect had clearly given way to the romantic appeal of the quiet moon. I, too, was enjoying the sense of peace but I was still acutely conscious of the unpleasantness of the night's proceedings ; and a certain envy took hold of me at this youth's capacity to concentrate on the attractive shadow of distasteful things. There was a heavy, musty smell over all this part of the

trench, the smell of a dead Turk lying just over
the parapet, and it occurred to me, maliciously,
to wake Harry from his dreams, and bring
home to him the reality of things.

' Funny smell you 've got here, Harry,' I
said ; ' know what it is ? '

' Yes, it 's cactus or amaryllis, or one of
those funny plants they have here, isn't it ?
I read about it in the papers.'

This was too much. ' It 's a dead Turk,'
I told him, with a wicked anticipation of the
effect I should produce.

The effect, however, was not what I expected.

' No ! ' said Harry, with obvious elation.
' Let 's find him.'

Forthwith he swarmed over the parapet,
full of life again, nosed about till he found
the reeking thing, and gazed on it with undis-
guised interest. No sign of horror or disgust
could I detect in him. Yet it was not pure
ghoulishness ; it was simply the boy's greed
for experience and the savour of adventure—
his first dead Turk. Anyhow, my experiment
had failed ; and I found that I was glad. But
when I was leaving him for the next platoon,
he was lying down for a little sleep on the dirty
floor of the trench, and as he flashed his electric
torch over the ground, I saw several small
white objects writhing in the dust. The company commander whom we had relieved had

told me how under all these trenches the Turks and the French had buried many of their dead, and in a moment of nauseating insight I knew that these things were the maggots which fed upon their bodies.

'Harry,' I said, 'you can't sleep there; look at those things!' And I told him what they were.

'Rubbish,' he said, 'they're glow-worms resting.'

Well, then I left him. But that's how he was in those days.

III

SO many men have written descriptions of trench life in France; there have been so many poems, plays, and speeches about it that the majority of our nation must have a much clearer mental picture of life on the Western Front than they have of life at the Savoy, or life in East Ham. But the Gallipoli Peninsula was never part of the Western Front, and no man came back from that place on leave; lucky, indeed, if he came at all. The campaign was never, for obvious reasons, an important item in official propaganda, and the various non-official agencies which now bring home the war to Streatham had not begun to articulate when the campaign came to an end. And so neither Streatham nor any one else knew anything about it. And though for a soldier to speak, however distantly, of the details of trench life in France, is now in some circles considered a solecism equivalent to the talking of 'shop,' I hope I may still without offence make some brief reference to the trenches of the Peninsula. For, in truth, it was all very different. Above all, from dawn to dawn it was genuine infantry warfare. In France, apart from full-dress attacks, an infantryman may live for many months without once firing his rifle, or running the remotest risk of death by a rifle bullet. Patiently he tramps, and watches, and digs, and is shelled, clinging fondly to his rifle night and day, but seldom or never in a position to use it ; so that in the stagnant days of the past he came to look upon it as a mere part of his equipment, like his water-bottle, only heavier and less comforting ; and in real emergencies fumbled stupidly with the unfamiliar mechanism. This was true for a long time of the normal, or ' peace-time,' sectors of France.

But in those hill-trenches of Gallipoli the Turk and the Gentile fought with each other all day with rifle and bomb, and in the evening crept out and stabbed each other in the dark. There was no release from the strain of watching and listening and taking thought. The Turk was always on higher ground ; he knew every inch of all those valleys and vineyards and scrub-strewn slopes ; and he had an uncanny accuracy of aim. Moreover, many of his men had the devotion of fanatics, which inspired them to lie out behind our lines, with stores of food enough to last out their ammunition, certain only of their own ultimate destruction, but content to lie there and pick off the infidels till they too died. They were very brave men. But the Turkish snipers were not

confined to the madmen who were caught
disguised as trees in the broad daylight and
found their way into the picture papers.
Every trench was full of snipers, less theatrical
but no less effective. And in the night they
crept out with inimitable stealth and lay close
in to our lines, killing our sentries, and chipping
away our crumbling parapets.

So the sniping was terrible. In that first
week we lost twelve men each day ; they fell
without a sound in the early morning as they
stood up from their cooking at the brazier, fell
shot through the head, and lay snoring horribly
in the dust ; they were sniped as they came up
the communication trench with water, or
carelessly raised their heads to look back at
the ships in the bay ; and in the night there
were sudden screams where a sentry ha i moved
his head too often against the moon. If a
periscope were raised, however furtively, it
was shivered in an instant ; if a man peered
over himself, he was dead. Far back in the
Reserve Lines or at the wells, where a man
thought himself hidden from view, the sniper
saw and killed him. All along the line were
danger posts where many had been hit ; these
places became invested with a peculiar awe,
and as you came to them the men said, ' Keep
low here, sir,' in a reverential whisper, as
though the Turk could hear them. Indeed, so

uncanny were many of the deaths, that some men said the Turk could see impossibly through the walls of the trench, and crouched nervously in the bottom. All the long communication trenches were watched, and wherever a head or a moving rifle showed at a gap a bullet came with automatic regularity. Going down a communication trench alone a man would hear the tap of these bullets on the parapet following him along, and break into a half-hysterical run in the bright sunlight to get away from this unnatural pursuit ; for such it seemed to him to be.

The fire seemed to come from all angles ; and units bitterly accused their neighbours of killing their men when it seemed impossible that any Turk could have fired the shot.

For a little, then, this sniping was thoroughly on the men's nerves. Nothing in their training had prepared them for it. They hated the ' blinded ' feeling it produced ; it was demoralizing always to be wondering if one's head was low enough, always to walk with a stoop ; it was tiring to be always taking care ; and it was very dangerous to relax that care for a moment. Something had to be done ; and the heavy, methodical way in which these Tynesiders of ours learned to counter and finally overcome the sniper, is characteristic of the nation's effort throughout this war.

The Turks were natural soldiers, fighting in
their own country ; more, they were natural
scouts. Our men were ponderous, uncouth
pitmen from Tyneside and the Clyde. But we
chose out a small body of them who could
shoot better than their fellows, and called them
snipers, and behold they *were* snipers. We gave
them telescopes, and periscopes, and observers,
and set them in odd corners, and told them to
snipe. And by slow degrees they became
interested and active and expert, and killed
many Turks. The third time we came to those
trenches we could move about with comparative
freedom.

In all this Harry took a leading part, for
the battalion scout officer was one of the first
casualties, and Harry, who had had some
training as a scout in the ranks, was appointed
in his place. In this capacity he was in charge
of the improvised snipers, and all day moved
about the line from post to post, encouraging
and correcting. All this he did with characteristic energy and enthusiasm, and tired
himself out with long wanderings in the scorching sun. In those trenches all movement was
an intense labour. The sun blazed always
into the suffocating ditch, where no breath
of air came ; the men not on duty lay huddled
wherever they could steal an inch of shade,
with the flies crawling about their eyes and

open mouths. Progress was a weary routine
of squeezing past men, or stepping over men,
or running into men round corners, as one
stooped to escape death. In little niches in
the wall were mess-tins boiling over box-wood
fires, so that the eyes smarted from their smoke,
and the air was full of the hot fumes ; and
everywhere was the stuffy smell of human flesh.
In the heat of the day these things produced
in the healthiest man a fretting irritation and
fatigue : to a frail, sensitive youth like Harry
his day-long rambles must have been torture ;
but though he too became touchy he pursued
his task with determination, and would not be
tempted away. The rest of us, when not on
watch, lay torpid all the hot hours in the
shallow holes we had scratched behind the
trench, and called Company Headquarters.
These places were roofed only with the inevitable waterproof sheet, and, had there been any
serious shelling, would have been death-traps.
Into these dwellings came many strange
animals, driven from their nests among the
roots of the scrub—snakes, lizards, and hideous
centipedes. Large, clumsy, winged things,
which some said were locusts, fell into the
trench, and for a few hours strove vainly to
leap out again till they were trampled to death ;
they had the colour of ivory, and shone with
bright tints in the sun like shot silk. The men

found tortoises derelict in near shell-holes, and set them to walk in the trench, and they too wandered sadly about till they disappeared, no man knew where. The flies were not yet at full strength, but they were very bad ; and all day we wrestled with thirst. He was a lucky man who could sleep in the daylight hours, and when the cool evening came, beckoning him to sleep, he must rise and bestir himself for the work of the night.

Then all the line hummed with life again, with the cleaning of rifles thick with heavy dust, and the bustle of men making ready to ' Stand to Arms.' Now, indeed, could a man have slept, when all the pests of the day had been exorcized by the cool dusk, and the bitter cold of the midnight was not yet come. But there was no sleep for any man, only watching and digging and carrying and working and listening. And so soon as Achi Baba was swathed in shadow, and the sun well down behind the westward islands, the Turk began his evening fusillade of rapid fire. This was an astonishing thing. Night after night at this hour every man in his trench must have blazed away till his rifle would do its work no more. ' Rapid fire ' has been a speciality of the Turkish infantryman since the days of Plevna, and he excels in it. Few English units could equal his performance for ten minutes ; but the Turk

kept up the same sustained deafening volume
of fire for hours at a stretch, till the moon came
up and allayed his fears.   For it was an exhibition of nervousness as well as musketry :
fearful of a stealthy assault in the dark, he
would not desist till he could see well across
his own wire.   Captured orders by the
Turkish High Command repeatedly forbade
this reckless expenditure of ammunition, and
sometimes for two nights he would restrain
himself, but in the early days never for more.
Our policy was to lie down in the trench, and
think sardonically of the ammunition he was
wasting ; but even this was not good for men's
minds.   Most of the fire was high and whizzed
over into the gullies, but many hundreds of all
those thousands of bullets hit the parapet.
There was a steady, reiterant rap of them on
the sand-bags, very irritating to the nerves, and
bits of the parapet splashed viciously into the
trench over the crouching men.   In that
tornado of sound a man must shout to make
himself heard by his friends, and this produced
in his mind an uncomfortable sense of isolation ;
he seemed cut off from humanity, and brooded
secretly to himself.   Safe he might be in that
trench, but he could not long sit alone in that
tempestuous security without imagining himself in other circumstances—climbing up the
parapet—leaving the trench—walking into

THAT. So on the few murky nights when the moon would not show herself but peeped temptingly from behind large bolsters of cloud, so that even the Turks diminished their fire, and then with a petulant crescendo continued, men lay in the dust and prayed for the moon to come. So demoralizing was this fire that it was not easy to induce even sentries to keep an effective watch. Not unnaturally, they did not like lifting their heads to look over, even for the periodical peeps which were insisted upon. An officer on his rounds would find them standing on the firestep with their heads well below the parapet, but gazing intently into the heart of a sand-bag, with the air of a man whóm no movement of the enemy can escape. The officer must then perform the melancholy rite of 'showing the men how safe it is.' This consisted in climbing up to the firestep, and exposing an immoderate amount of his head ; gazing deliberately at the Turks, and striving to create an impression of indifference and calm. He then jumped down, shouting cheerily, 'That's the way, Thompson,' and walked off, thanking God. Personally I did not like this duty. At the best it was an hypocrisy. For the reluctance of the officer to look over was no less acute than the man's ; and it was one thing to look for a moment or two and pass on, and another to stand there and repeat the process at brief intervals. Officers performed this rite according to their several characters : Eustace, for example, with a cynical grin which derided, with equal injustice, both himself and his action ; he was notably courageous, and his nonchalance on the parapet would have been definitely reassuring to the nervous sentry. But his expression and attitude said clearly : ' This is all damned nonsense, my good man ; *you* don't like standing up here, neither do I, and neither of us is deceiving the other at all.' Burnett did it with genuine and ill-concealed distaste, too hasty to be convincing. Harry, alone, did it with a gallant abandon, like a knight throwing down his challenge to the enemy ; and he alone can have been really inspiring to the reluctant sentry. He had a keen dramatic instinct, and I think in these little scenes rather enjoyed the part of the unperturbed hero calming the timorous herd. Watching him once or twice I wondered how much was acting and how much real fearlessness ; if it was acting he was braver then than most of us—but I think it was the other just then.

There were five or six hours between the end of the rapid fire and the ' Stand to ' before dawn. During these hours three of the company officers were always on duty. We split the time in two, and it was a weary three hours patrolling the still trench, stumbling over sleeping men, sprawled out like dead in the moonlight, and goading the tired sentries to watchfulness. Terrible was the want of sleep. The men fell asleep with their heads against the iron loopholes, and, starting up as the officer shook them, swore that they had never nodded. Only by constant movement could the officer be sure even of himself ; he dared not sit for a moment or lean in the corner of the traverse, though all his limbs ached for rest, lest he, too, be found snoring at his post, and he and all his men be butchered in their guilty sleep. And so he drags his sore feet ceaselessly backwards and forwards, marvelling at the stillness and the stars and the strange musky night smell which has crept out of the earth. Far away he can see the green lights of a hospital ship, and as he looks they begin to move and dwindle slowly into the distance, for she is going home ; and he thinks of the warmth and light and comfort in that ship, and follows her wistfully with his eyes till she is gone. Turning back he sees a sentry, silent above him ; he, too, is watching the ship, and each man knows the other's thoughts, but they do not speak.

At last comes the officer relieving him, cold and irritable from his brief sleep. He is a little late, and they compare watches resentfully ; and unless they be firm friends, at that

moment they may hate each other. But the
one who is relieved goes down to the dug-out
in the support line, a little jauntily now,
though his feet are painful, feeling already that
he could watch many hours more. And
suddenly the moon is beautiful, and the stars
are friendly—for he is going to sleep. But
when he comes to the little narrow hole which
is the dug-out, there are two officers already
filling most of the floor, noisily asleep. One
of them is lying on his waterproof sheet : he
tugs angrily at it, but it is caught in something
and will not come away. He shakes the man,
but he does not wake. Too tired to persevere
he lies down awkwardly in the crooked space
which is left between the legs and arms and
equipment of the others. He draws his meagre
trench-coat over his body, and pulls his knees
up that they, too, may be covered ; there is
nothing over his feet, and already they are cold.
His head he rests on a rough army haversack.
In the middle of it there is a hard knob, a
soap-tin, or a book, or a tin of beef. For a
little he lies uncomfortably like this, hoping
for sleep ; his ear is crushed on the hard pillow ;
there is something lumpy under his hip. He
knows that he ought to get up and rearrange
himself—but the effort is too much. At last
he raises himself on his elbow and tugs at the
towel in his haversack to make him a pillow ;

the strap of the haversack is fastened, and the towel will not emerge. He unfastens the haversack, and in desperation pulls out the whole of its contents with the towel. His toothbrush and his sponge and his diary are scattered in the dust. Some of the pages of the diary are loose, and if he leaves it they will be lost ; he feels in the darkness for his electric torch, and curses because he cannot find it. He has lent it to the damned fool who relieved him. Why can't people have things of their own ?

Painfully groping he gathers his belongings and puts them, one by one, in the haversack, arranging his towel on the top. His elbow is sore with leaning on it, but the pillow is ready. Lying down again he falls quickly to sleep. Almost at once there is a wild din in his dreams. Rapid fire again. Springing up, he rushes into the trench with the others. It is an attack. Who is attacking ? The men in the trench know nothing. It started on the right, they say, and now the whole line is ablaze again with this maddening rifle-fire. Running back to the dug-out he gropes in the wreckage of coats and equipment for his belt and revolver. He must hurry to the front line to take charge of his platoon. There are no telephones to the firing-line. What the hell is happening ? When he is halfway up the communication trench, cannoning into the walls in his haste and weariness, the firing suddenly stops. It was a wild panic started by the Senegalese holding the line on our right. Damn them—black idiots!

He goes back swearing with the other officers, and they lie down anyhow; it is too late now to waste time on fussy arrangements. When he wakes up again there is already a hint of light in the east. It is the 'Stand to Arms' before dawn. His feet are numb and painful with cold, his limbs are cramped and aching, and his right forearm has gone to sleep. The flesh of his legs is clammy, and sticks to the breeches he has lived and slept in for five days : he longs for a bath. Slowly with the others he raises himself and gropes weakly in the muddle of garments on the floor for his equipment. He cannot find his revolver. Burnett has lost his belt, and mutters angrily to himself. All their belongings are entangled together in the narrow space; they disengage them without speaking to each other. Each one is in a dull coma of endurance; for the moment their spirit is at its lowest ebb; it is the most awful moment of warfare. In a little they will revive, but just now they cannot pretend to bravery or cheerfulness, only curse feebly and fumble in the darkness.

They go out into the trench and join their

platoons. The N.C.O.'s are still shaking and
bullying the men still asleep ; some of these are
almost senseless, and can only be roused by
prolonged physical violence. The officer braces
himself for his duties, and by and by all the men
are more or less awake and equipped, though
their heads droop as they sit, and their neighbours nudge them into wakefulness as the
officer approaches. Mechanically he fills and
lights a pipe, and takes a cautious sip at his
water-bottle ; the pipe turns his empty
stomach, and a sickly emptiness assails him.
He knocks out the pipe and peers over the
parapet. It is almost light now, but a thin
mist hides the Turkish trench. His face is
greasy and taut with dirt, and the corners of
his eyes are full of dust ; his throat is dry, and
there is a loathsome stubble on his chin, which
he fingers absently, pulling at the long hairs.

Steadily the light grows and grows, and the
men begin to chatter, and suddenly the sun
emerges over the corner of Achi Baba, and
life and warmth come back to the numb souls
of all these men. ' Stand to ' is over ; but
as the men tear off their hateful equipment
and lean their rifles against the wall of the
trench there is a sudden burst of shelling on the
right. Figures appear running on the skyline. They are against the light, and the shapes
are dark, but there seems to be a dirty blue in

their uniforms. No one quite knows how the line runs up there; it is a salient. The figures must be Turks attacking the French. The men gape over the parapet. The officer gapes. It is nothing to do with them. Then he remembers what he is for, and tells his men excitedly to fire at the figures. Some of the men have begun cooking their breakfast, and are with difficulty seduced from their task. A spasmodic fire opens on the running figures. It is hard to say where they are running, or what they are doing. The officer is puzzled. It is his first glimpse of battle, and he feels that a battle should be simple and easy to understand. The officer of the next platoon comes along. He is equally ignorant of affairs, but he thinks the figures are French, attacking the Turks. They, too, wear blue. The first officer rushes down the line telling the men to 'cease fire.' The men growl and go back to their cooking. It is fairly certain that none of them hit any of the distant figures, but the officer is worried. Why was nobody told what was to happen? What is it all about? He has been put in a false position. Presently a belated chit arrives to say that the French were to attack at sunrise, but the attack was a fiasco and is postponed.

And now all the air is sickly with the smell of cooking, and the dry wood crackles in every

corner; little wisps of smoke go straight up
in the still air. All the Peninsula is beautiful
in the sunlight, and wonderful to look upon
against the dark blue of the sea; the dew
sparkles on the scrub; over the cypress grove
comes the first aeroplane, humming contentedly. Another day has begun; the officer
goes down whistling to wash in a bucket.

IV

SUCH was life in the line at that time. But I should make the soldier's almost automatic reservation, that it might have been worse. There might have been heavy shelling; but the shelling on the trenches was negligible— then; there might have been mud, but there was not. And eight such days might have left Harry Penrose quite unaffected in spirit, in spite of his physical handicaps, by reason of his extraordinary vitality and zest. But there were two incidents before we went down which did affect him, and it is necessary that they should be told.

On the fifth day in the line he did a very brave thing—brave, at least, in the popular sense, which means that many another man would not have done that thing. To my mind, a man is brave only in proportion to his knowledge and his susceptibility to fear; the standard of the mob, the standard of the official military mind, is absolute; there are no fine shades—no account of circumstance and temperament is allowed—and perhaps this is inevitable. Most men would say that Harry's deed was a brave one. I have said so myself —but I am not sure.

Eighty to a hundred yards from one section of our line was a small stretch of Turkish trench, considerably in advance of their main line. From this trench a particularly harassing fire was kept up, night and day, and the Brigade Staff considered that it should be captured. High officers in shirt sleeves and red hats looked long and wisely at it through periscopes ; colonels and adjutants and subalterns and sergeants stood silent and respectful while the great men pondered. The great men then turned round with the air of those who make profound decisions, and announced that ' You ought to be able to " enfilade " it from " over there," ' or ' I suppose they " enfilade " you from there.' The term ' enfilade ' invariably occurred somewhere in these dicta, and in the listeners' minds there stirred the suspicion that the Great Ones had not been looking at the right trench ; if indeed they had focused the unfamiliar instrument so as to see anything at all. But the decision was made ; and for the purposes of a night attack it was important to know whether the trench was held strongly at night, or occupied only by a few busy snipers. Harry was ordered to reconnoitre the trench with two scouts.

The night was pitch black, with an unusual absence of stars. The worst of the rapid fire was over, but there was a steady spit and crackle of bullets from the Turks, and especially from the little trench opposite. Long afterwards, in France, he told me that he would never again dream of going out on patrol in the face of such a fire. But to-night it did not occur to him to delay his expedition. The profession of scouting made a special appeal to the romantic side of him ; the prospect of some real, practical scouting was exciting. According to the books much scouting was done under heavy fire, but according to the books, and in the absence of any experience to the contrary, it was probable that the careful scout would not be killed. Then why waste time ? (All this I gathered indirectly from his account of the affair.) Two bullets smacked into the parapet by his head as he climbed out of the dark sap and wriggled forward into the scrub ; but even these did not give him pause. Only while he lay and waited for the two men to follow did he begin to realize how many bullets were flying about. The fire was now really heavy, and when I heard that Harry had gone out, I was afraid. But he as yet was only faintly surprised. The Colonel had sent him out ; the Colonel had said the Turks fired high, and if you kept low you were quite safe—and he ought to know. This was a regular thing in warfare, and must be done. So on like reptiles into the darkness, dragging with hands

and pushing with knees. Progress in the
orthodox scout fashion was surprisingly slow
and exhausting. The scrub tickled and
scratched your face, the revolver in your hands
caught in the roots ; the barrel must be choked
with dust. Moreover, it was impossible to see
anything at all, and the object of a reconnaissance being to see something, this was per-
plexing. Even when the frequent flares went
up and one lay pressed to the earth, one's
horizon was the edge of a tuft of scrub five
yards away. This always looked like the
summit of some commanding height ; but
labouring thither one saw by the next flare
only another exactly similar horizon beyond.
So must the beetle feel, wandering in the
rugged spaces of a well-kept lawn. It was
long before Harry properly understood this
phenomenon ; and by then his neck was stiff
and aching from lying flat and craning his head
back to see in front. But after an hour of
crawling the ground sloped down a little, and
now they could see the sharp, stabbing flashes
from the rifles of the snipers in the little trench
ahead of them. Clearly they were only snipers,
for the flashes came from only eight or nine
particular spots, spaced out at intervals. *Now*
the scouts glowed with the sense of achievement as they watched. They had found out.
Never again could Harry have lain like that,

naked in the face of those near rifles, coldly
calculating and watching, without an effort of
real heroism.   On this night he did it easily
—confident, unafraid.   Elated with his little
success, something prompted him to go farther
and confirm his deductions.   He whispered to
his men to lie down in a fold of the ground,
and crept forward to the very trench itself,
aiming at a point midway between two flashes.
There was no wire in front of the trench, but
as he saw the parapet looming like a mountain
close ahead, he began to realize what a mad
fool he was, alone and helpless within a few
yards of the Turks, an easy mark in the light
of the next flare.   But he would not go back,
and squirming on worked his head into a gap
in the parapet, and gazed into a vast blackness.
This he did with a wild incautiousness, the
patience of the true scout overcome by his
anxiety to do what he intended as soon as
possible.   The Turks' own rifles had drowned
the noise of his movements, and providentially
no flare went up till his body was against the
parapet.   When at length the faint wavering
light began and swelled into sudden brilliance,
he could see right into the trench, and when
the shadows chased each other back into its
depths as the light fell, he lay marvelling at
his own audacity : so impressed was he by
the wonder of his exploit that he was incapable

of making any intelligent observations, other than the bald fact that there were no men in that part of the trench. He was still waiting for another flare when there was a burst of rapid fire from our own line a little to the right. Suddenly he realized that B Company *did not know he was out*; C Company knew, but in his haste he had forgotten to see that the others were informed before he left, as he had arranged to do with the Colonel. He and his scouts would be shot by B Company. Obsessed with this thought he turned and scrambled breathlessly back to the two waiting men. God knows why he wasn't seen and sniped; and his retirement must have been very noisy, for as he reached the others all the snipers in the trench opened fire feverishly together. Harry and his men, who were cold with waiting, wriggled blindly back; they no longer pretended to any deliberation or cunning, but having come to no harm so far were not seriously anxious about themselves; only it seemed good to go back now. But after a few yards one of the men, Trower, gave a scream of agony and cried out, ' I 'm hit, I 'm hit.'

In that moment, Harry told me, all the elation and pride of his exploit ebbed out of him. A sick disgust with himself and everything came over him. Williams, the other scout, lay between him and Trower, who was

now moaning horribly in the darkness. For
a moment Harry was paralysed ; he lay there,
saying feebly, ' Where are you hit ?   Where
is he hit, Williams ?   Where are you hit ? '
When at last he got to his side, the man was
almost unconscious with pain, but he had
managed to screech out ' Both legs.'   In fact,
he had been shot through the femoral artery
and one leg was broken.   In that blackness
skilled hands would have had difficulty in
bandaging any wound ; Harry and Williams
could not even tell where the wound was, for
all his legs were wet and sticky with blood.
But both of them were fumbling and scratching
at their field-dressings for some moments
before they realized this.   Then they started
to take the man in, half dragging, half carrying him.   At every movement the man shrieked
in agony.   When they stood up to carry him
bodily, he screamed so piercingly that the
storm of bullets was immediately doubled
about them. When they lay down and
dragged him he screamed less, but progress
was impossibly slow.   And now it seemed that
there were Turks in the open scrub about them,
for there were flashes and loud reports at
strangely close quarters.   The Turks could not
see the miserable little   party, but Trower's
screams were an easy guide.   Then Harry
bethought him of the little medical case in his

breast-pocket where, with needles and aspirin
and plaster and pills, was a small phial of
morphine tablets. For Trower's sake and
their own, his screaming must be stilled.
Tearing open his pocket he fumbled at the
elastic band round the case. The little phial
was smaller than the rest; he knew where it
lay. But the case was upside-down; all the
phials seemed the same size. Trembling, he
pulled out the cork and shook out one of the
tablets into his hand; a bullet cracked like
a whip over his head; the tablet fell in the
scrub. He got another out and passed it over
to Williams. Williams' hand was shaking, and
he dropped it. Harry groaned. The next
two were safely transferred and pressed into
Trower's mouth: he did not know how strong
they were, but he remembered vaguely seeing
' One or two ' on the label, and at that black
moment the phrase came curiously into his
head, ' As ordered by the doctor.' Trower
was quieter now, and this made the other two
a little calmer. Harry told me he was now so
cool that he could put the phial back carefully
in the case and return them to his pocket;
even, from sheer force of habit, he buttoned
up the pocket. But when they moved off
they realized with a new horror that they were
lost. They had come out originally from the
head of a long sap; in the darkness and the

excitement they had lost all sense of direction,
and had missed the sap. Probably they were
not more than fifty yards from friends, but
they might be moving parallel to the sap or
parallel to the front line, and that way they
might go on indefinitely. They could not drag
their wretched burden with them indefinitely ;
so Harry sent Williams to find the trench, and
lay throbbing by the wounded man. No one
who has not been lost in the pitchy dark in No
Man's Land can understand how easy it is to
arrive at that condition, and the intense feeling
of helplessness it produces. That solitary wait
of Harry's must have been terrible ; for he had
time now to ponder his position. Perhaps
Williams would not find the trench ; perhaps
he, too, would be hit ; perhaps he would not
be able to find the scouts again. What should
they do then ? Anything was possible in this
awful darkness, with these bullets cracking
and tearing about him. Perhaps he would
be killed himself. Straining his ears he fancied
he could hear the rustle of creeping men, any
moment he expected a rending blow on his own
tender body. But his revolver had been
dropped in the dragging of Trower. He could
do nothing—only try to bind up the poor legs
again. Poor Harry ! as he lay there bandaging
his scout, he noticed that the lad had stopped
moaning, and said to himself that his morphine

tablets had done their work. That was something, anyhow. But the man was already dead.
He could not have lived for ten minutes, the
doctor told me. And when Williams at last
returned, trailing a long string from the sap,
it was a dead man they brought painfully into
the trench and handed over gently to the
stretcher-bearers.

I was in the sap when they came, and dragged
Harry away from it. And when they told him
he nearly cried.

II

The other incident is briefly told. On our
last day in the line Harry's platoon were
working stealthily in the hot sun at a new
section of trench connecting two saps, and
some one incautiously threw a little new-
turned earth over the parapet. The Turks,
who seldom molested any of the regular,
established trenches with shell-fire, but hotly
resented the making of new ones, opened fire
with a light high-velocity gun of the whizz-
bang type. This was our first experience of
the weapon, and the first experience of a whizz-
bang is very disturbing. The long shriek of
the ordinary shell encourages the usually futile
hope that by ducking one may avoid destruction. With the whizz-bang there is no hope,

for there is no warning ; the sound and the
shell arrive almost simultaneously. Harry's
platoon did not like these things. The first
three burst near but short of the trench, filling
the air with fumes ; the fourth hit and removed
most of the parapet of one bay. Harry, hurry-
ing along to the place, found the four men there
considerably surprised, crouching in the corners
and gazing stupidly at the yawning gap. It
was undesirable, if not impossible, to rebuild
the parapet during daylight, so he moved them
into the next bay. He then went along the
trench to see that all the men had ceased work.
He heard two more shells burst behind him as
he went. On his way back two men rushing
round a corner—two men with white faces
smeared with black and a little blood—almost
knocked him down ; they were speechless.
He went through the bay which had been blown
in ; it was silent, empty ; the bay beyond was
silent too, save for the buzzing of a thousand
flies. In it he had left eight men ; six of
them were lying dead. Two had marvellously
escaped. The first whizz-bang had blown
away the parapet ; the second, following
immediately after, had passed miraculously
through the hole, straight into the trench—
a piece of astounding bad luck or good gunnery.
The men could not be buried till dusk, and we
left them there.

Two hours later, as we sat under a waterproof sheet and talked quietly of this thing, there came an engineer officer wandering along the trench. He had come, crouching, through those two shattered and yawning bays : he was hot and very angry. ' Why the hell don't you bury those Turks ? ' he said, ' they must have been there for weeks ! ' This is the kind of charge which infuriates the soldier at any time ; and we did not like the added suggestion that those six good men of the 14th Platoon were dead Turks. We told him they were Englishmen, dead two hours. ' But, my God, man,' he said, ' they're black ! ' We led him back, incredulous, to the place.

When we got there we understood. Whether from the explosion or the scorching sun in that airless place, I know not, but those six men were, as he said, black—black and reeking and hideous—and the flies . . . !

Harry and I crouched at the end of that bay, truly unable to believe our eyes. I hope I may never again see such horror as was in Harry's face. They were men of his platoon, and he knew them, as an officer should. After the explosion, there had been only four whom he could surely identify. Now there was not one.

In two hours. . . .

•   •   •   •   •

I do not wish to labour this or any similar episode. I have seen many worse things; every soldier has. In a man's history they are important only in their effect upon him, and the effect they have is determined by many things—by his experience, and his health, and his state of mind. But if you are to understand what I may call the battle-psychology of a man, as I want you to understand Harry's, you must not ignore particular incidents. For in this respect the lives of soldiers are not uniform; though they may live in the same regiment and fight in the same battles, the experiences which matter come to them diversely—to some crowded and overwhelming, to others by kind and delicate degrees. And so do their spirits develop.

These two incidents following so closely upon each other had a most unhappy cumulative effect on Harry. His night's scouting, in spite of its miserable end, had not perceptibly dimmed his romantic notions; it had been an adventure, and from a military point of view a successful adventure. The Colonel had been pleased with the reconnaissance, as such. But the sight of his six poor men, lying black and beastly in that sunlit hole, had killed the ' Romance of War ' for him. Henceforth it must be a necessary but disgusting business, to be endured, like a dung-hill. But this, in the end, was inevitable ; with all soldiers it is only a matter of time, though for a boy of Harry's temperament it was an ill chance that it should come so soon.

What was more serious was this: the two incidents had revived, in a most malignant form, his old distrust of his own competence. I found that he was brooding over this—accusing himself, quite wrongly, I think, of being responsible for the death of seven men. He had bungled the scouting ; he had recklessly attracted attention to the party, and Trower, not he, had paid for it. He had moved four men into a bay where four others already were, and six of them had been killed. I tried hard to persuade him, not quite honestly, that he had done absolutely the right thing. In scouting, of all things, I told him, a man *must* take chances ; and the matter of the two whizz-bangs was sheer bad luck. It was no good ; he was a fool—a failure. Unconsciously, the Colonel encouraged this attitude. For, thinking that Harry's nerve might well have been shaken by his first experience, he would not let him go out on patrol again on our next ' tour ' in the line. I think he was quite mistaken in this view, for the boy did not even seem to realize how narrow his own escapes had been, so concerned was he about his lost men. Nor did this explanation of the Colonel's

veto even occur to him.   Rather it confirmed
him in his distrust of himself, for it seemed to
him that the Colonel, too, must look upon him
as a bungler, a waster of men's lives.

All this was very bad, and I was much afraid
of what the reaction might be.   But there was
one bright spot.   So far he only distrusted
his military capacity ; there was no sign of his
distrusting his own courage.   I prayed that
that might not follow.

V

MID-JUNE came with all its plagues and fevers and irritable distresses. Life in the rest-camp became daily more tormenting. There set in a steady wind from the north-east which blew all day down the flayed rest-areas of the Peninsula, raising great columns of blinding, maddening dust. It was a hot, parching wind, which in no way mitigated the scorch of the sun, and the dust it brought became a definite enemy to human peace. It pervaded everything. It poured into every hole and dug-out, and filtered into every man's belongings ; it formed a gritty sediment in water and tea, it passed into a man with every morsel of food he ate and scraped and tore at his inside. It covered his pipe so that he could not even smoke with pleasure ; it lay in a thick coating on his face so that he looked like a wan ghost, paler than disease had made him. It made the cleaning of his rifle a too, too frequent farce ; it worked under his breeches, and gathered at the back of his knees, chafing and torturing him ; and if he lay down to sleep in his hole it swept in billows over his face, or men passing clumsily above kicked great showers upon him. Sleep was not possible in the rest-camps while that wind blew. But indeed there were many things which made rest in the rest-camps impossible. Few more terrible plagues can have afflicted British troops than the flies of Gallipoli. In May, by comparison, there were none. In June they came by armies ; in July by multitudes. Most Englishmen have lain down some gentle summer day to doze on a shaded lawn and found that one or two persistent flies have destroyed the repose of the afternoon ; many women have turned sick at the sight of a blowfly in their butcher's shop. Let them imagine a semitropical sun in a place where there is little or no shade, where sanitary arrangements are less than primitive, where, in spite of all precautions, there are scraps of bacon and sugar and tealeaves lying everywhere in the dust, and every man has his little daily store of food somewhere near him, where there are dead bodies and the carcases of mules easily accessible to the least venturesome fly—let them read for ' one ' fly a hundred, a thousand, a million, and even then they will not exaggerate the horror of that plague.

Under it the disadvantages of a sensitive nature and a delicate upbringing were easy to see. An officer lies down in the afternoon to sleep in his hole. The flies cluster on his face. Patiently, at first, he brushes them away, with a drill-like mechanical movement of his hand ; by-and-by he does it angrily ; his temper is going. He covers his face with a handkerchief ; it is distressingly hot, but at least he may have some rest. The flies settle on his hand, on his neck, on the bare part of his leg. Even there the feel of them is becoming a genuine torment. They creep under the handkerchief ; there is one on his lip, another buzzing about his eye. Madly he tears off the handkerchief and lashes out, waving it furiously till the air is free. The flies gather on the walls of the dug-out, on the waterproof sheet, and watch ; they are waiting motionless till he lies down again. He throws his coat over his bare knees and lies back. The torment begins again. It is unendurable. He gets up, cursing, and goes out ; better to walk in the hot sun or sit under the olive-tree in the windy dust.

But look into the crowded ditches of the men. Some of them are fighting the same fight, hands moving and faces twitching, like the flesh of horses, automatically. But most of them lie still, not asleep, but in a kind of dogged artificial insensibility. The flies crowd on their faces ; they swarm about their eyes, and crawl unmolested about their open mouths. It is a horrible sight, but those men are lucky.

Then there was always a great noise in the camp, for men would be called for from Head-quarters at the end of it or orders passed down, and so great was the wind and the noise of the French guns and the Turkish shells, that these messages had to be bawled from man to man. The men grew lazy from sheer weariness of these messages, so that they were mutilated as they came and had to be repeated ; and there was this babel always. The men, too, like the officers, became irritable with each other, and wrangled incessantly over little things ; only the officers argued quietly and bitterly, and the men shouted oaths at each other and filthy epithets. There was only a yard between the holes of the officers and the holes of the men, and their raucous quarrelling grated on nerves already sensitive from the trials of the day, and the officer came near to cursing his own men ; and that is bad.

So there was no rest to be had in the camp during the day ; and at night we marched out in long columns to dig in the whispering gullies, or unload ships on the beach. There were many of these parties, and we were much overworked, as all infantry units invariably are ; and only at long intervals there came an evening when a man might lie down under the perfect stars and sleep all night undisturbed. Then indeed he had rest ; and when he woke to a sudden burst of shell-fire, lay quiet in his hole, too tired and dreamy to be afraid.

Dust and flies and the food and the water and our weakness joined forces against us, and dysentery raged. There were many who had never heard of the disease, and thought vaguely of the distemper of dogs. Those who had heard of it thought of it as something rather romantically Eastern, like the tsetse fly, and the first cases were invested with a certain mysterious distinction—especially as most of them were sent away. But it became universal ; everybody had it, and everybody could not be sent away. One man in a thousand went through that time untouched ; one in ten escaped with a slight attack. But the remainder lived permanently or intermittently in a condition which in any normal campaign would have long since sent them on stretchers to the base. The men could not be spared ; they stayed and endured and tottered at their work. Thus there was every circumstance to encourage infection and little to resist it. One by one the officers of D Company were stricken. The first stages were mildly unpleasant, encouraging that comfortable sense of martyrdom which belongs to a recognized but endurable complaint. As it grew worse, men became querulous but were still interested in themselves, and those not in the final stages discussed their symptoms,

emulously, disgustingly—still a little anxious
to be worse than their fellows.

In the worst stage there was no emulation,
only a dull misery of recurrent pain and lassitude
and disgust.   A man could not touch the coarse
food which was all we had ; or, if from sheer
emptiness he did, his sufferings were immediately
magnified.   Yet always he had a wild craving
for delicate food, and as he turned from the
sickening bacon in the gritty lid of his mess-tin,
conjured bright visions of lovely dainties
which might satisfy his longing and give him
back his strength.   So men prayed for parcels.
But when they came, or when some wanderer
came back from the Islands with a basket of
Grecian eggs, too often it was too late for the
sickest men, and their agonies were only
increased.   Scientific dieting was impossible.
They could only struggle on, for ever sick, yet
for ever on duty ; this was the awful thing.
When a man reached this stage, the army was
lucky indeed if it did not lose him ; he was
lucky himself if he did not die.   But so strong
is the human spirit and so patient the human
body, that most won through this phase to a
spasmodic existence of alternate sickness and
precarious health ;   and when they said to
themselves ' I am well,' and ate heartily, and
said to their companions ' This and that is what
you should do,' the disease gripped them again,

each time more violently. All this sapped the
strength of a man ; and finally there came a
terrible debility, a kind of paralysing lassitude,
when it needed a genuine flogging of the will for
him to lift himself and walk across the camp,
and his knees seemed permanently feeble, as if
a fever had just left him. Yet many endured
this condition for weeks and months till the
fever definitely took them. Some became so
weak that while they still tottered up to the line
and about their duties, they could not gratui-
tously drag themselves to the beach to bathe.
Then indeed were they far gone, for the evening
swims were the few paradisial moments of that
time. When the sun had but an hour to live,
and the wind and the dust and the flies were
already dwindling, we climbed down a cliff-
path where the Indians kept their sacred but
odorous goats. There was a fringe of rocks
under the cliffs where we could dive. There
we undressed, hot and grimy, lousy, thirsty,
and tired. Along the rocks solitary Indians
were kneeling towards Mecca. Some of the old
battered boats of the first landing were still
nosing the shore, and at a safe distance was a
dead mule. The troops did not come here but
waded noisily in the shallow water ; so all was
quiet, save for an occasional lazy shell from
Asia and the chunk-chunk of a patrol-boat.
The sea at this hour put on its most perfect blue,

and the foot-hills across the Straits were all
warm and twinkling in the late sun. So we
sat and drank in the strengthening breeze, and
felt the clean air on our contaminated flesh ;
and plunging luxuriously into the lovely water
forgot for a magical moment all our weariness
and disgust.

When a man could not do this, he was ill
indeed.

II

By this time we had found each other out.
We had discovered a true standard of right and
wrong ; we knew quite clearly now, some of us
for the first time, what sort of action was
' dirty,' and we were fairly clear how likely
each of us was to do such an action.   We knew
all our little weaknesses and most of our serious
flaws ;   under that olive-tree they could not
long be hid.   In the pleasant life of London or
Oxford.we had had no occasion to do anything
dishonourable or underhand ; in our relations
with other men we had not even wished to be
guilty of anything worse than mild unkindnesses
or consistent unpunctuality.   But behind the
footlights of Gallipoli we had found real burning
temptations ; and we had found our characters.
D Company on the whole was lucky, and had
stood the test well.   We knew that Burnett
was ' bogus ' ; but we knew that Williams of

A Company was incalculably more 'bogus';
we had stood in the dark sap at night and
reluctantly overheard the men of his company
speak of him.

But little weaknesses beget great irritations
in that life, and the intimate problems of com-
munal feeding were enough to search out all our
weaknesses.   We knew that some of us, though
courageous, were greedy ; that others, though
not greedy, were querulous about their food
and had a nasty habit of ' sticking out for their
rights ' : indeed, I think I developed this habit
myself. We had had trouble about parcels.
Parcels in theory were thrown into the common
stock of the mess : but Egerton and Burnett
never had parcels, and were by no means the
most delicate eaters of other people's dainties.
Harry and Hewett reserved some portion of
each parcel, a cake or a slab of chocolate, which
they ate furtively in their dug-outs, or shared
with each other in the dusk ; Burnett ostenta-
tiously endowed the mess with his entire stock,
but afterwards at every meal hinted sombrely
at the rapacity of those who had devoured it.
Harry and Hewett each made contributions to
the mess ; but Harry objected to the excessive
consumption of this food by Burnett, and
Hewett, who gave ungrudgingly to the rest of
us, had a similar reservation—never expressed
—as against Egerton. So all this matter of

food set in motion a number of antagonisms seldom or never articulate, but painfully perceptible at every meal.

The parcel question, I think, was one of the things which embittered the quarrel between Harry and Burnett. A parcel from home, to schoolboys and soldiers and prisoners and sailors and all homesick exiles, is the most powerful emblem of sentiment and affection. A man would willingly preserve its treasures for himself to gloat over alone, in no mere fleshly indulgence, but as a concrete expression of affection from the home for which he longs. This is not nonsense. He likes to undo the strings in the grubby hole which is his present home, and secretly become sentimental over the little fond packages and queer, loving thoughts which have composed it. And though in a generous impulse he may say to his companions, ' Come and eat this cake,' and see it in a moment disappear, it is hard for him not to think, ' My sister (or wife, or mother) made this *for me* ; they thought it would give *me* pleasure for many days. Already it is gone— would they not be hurt if they knew ? ' He feels that he has betrayed the tenderness of his home ; and though the giving of pleasure to companions he likes may overcome this feeling, the compulsory squandering of such precious pleasure on a man he despises calls up the worst bitterness of his heart. So was it between Harry and Burnett.

If, by the way, it be suggested that Burnett was entitled to feel the same sentimental jealousy about *his* parcels, I answer that Burnett's parcels came on his own order from the impersonal hand of Fortnum and Mason.

All of us were very touchy, very raw and fretful in that fevered atmosphere. Men who were always late in relieving another on watch, or unreasonably resented a minute's postponement of their relief, or never had any article of their own but for ever borrowed mess-tins and electric torches and note-books from more methodical people, or were overbearing to batmen, or shifted jobs on to other officers, or slunk off to bathe alone when they should have taken their sultry platoon—such men made enemies quickly. Between Eustace and Hewett, who had been good friends before and were to be good friends again, there grew up a slow animosity. Hewett was one of the methodical class of officer, Eustace was one of the persistent borrowers. Moreover, as I have said, he was a cynic, and he *would* argue. He had a contentious remark for every moment of the day; and though this tormented us all beyond bearing, Hewett was the only one with both the energy and the intellectual equipment to accept his challenges. So these two argued quietly

and fiercely in the hot noon or the blue
dusk, till the rest of us were weary of them
both, and the sound of Eustace's harsh tones
was an agony to the nerves. They were both
too consciously refined to lose their tempers
healthily, and when they reached danger-point,
Hewett would slink away like an injured animal
to his burrow. In this conflict Harry took no
speaking part, for while in spirit and affection
he was on Hewett's side, he paid intellectual
tribute to Eustace's conduct of the argument,
and listened as a rule in puzzled silence.
Eustace again was his cordial ally against Burnett
while Hewett had merely the indifference of
contempt for that officer.

So it was all a strange tangle of friendship
and animosity and good-nature and bitterness.
Yet on the surface, you understand, we lived
on terms of toleration and vague geniality ;
except for the disputations of Hewett and
Eustace there was little open disagreement.   In
the confined space of a company mess permanent
hostilities would make life impossible ; it is
only generals who are allowed to find that they
can no longer ' act with ' each other, and
resign : platoon commanders may come to the
same conclusion, but they have to go on acting.
And so openly we laughed and endured and
bore with each other.   Only there was always
this undertone of irritations and animosities

which, in the maddening conditions of our life, could never be altogether silenced, and might at any moment rise to a strangled scream.

Harry's appointment as Scout Officer was the first thing to set Burnett against Harry, though already many things had set Harry against Burnett. It had been commonly assumed, in view of Burnett's ' backwoods ' reputation, that he would succeed Martin as Scout Officer.   The Colonel's selection of Harry took us a little by surprise, though it only showed that the Colonel was a keener judge of character and ability than the rest of us.   No one, I think, was more genuinely pleased that Burnett was not to be Scout Officer than Burnett himself ; but in the interests of his ' dare-devil ' pretensions he had to affect an air of disappointment, and let it be known by grunts and shrugs and sour looks that he considered the choice of Harry to be an injury to himself and the battalion.   As far as Harry was concerned this resentment of Burnett's was more or less genuine, for his reluctance to take on the job did not prevent him being jealous of the man who did.

Then Burnett was one of the people who had nothing of his own, and seemed to regard Harry, as the youngest of us all, as the proper person to provide him with all the necessaries of life.   In those days we had no plates or

crockery, but ate and drank out of our scratched
and greasy mess-tins. Harry's mess-tin disappeared, and for three days he was compelled
to borrow from Hewett or myself—a tedious
and, to him, hateful business. One day Burnett had finished his meal a long way ahead
of any of us, and Harry, in the desperation of
hungry waiting, asked him for the loan of his
mess-tin. Automatically he looked at the
bottom of the tin, and there found his initials
inscribed. It was his own tin. Further, some
one had tried to scratch the initials out. Harry
kept his temper with obvious difficulty. Burnett
knew well that Harry had lost his mess-tin (we
were all sick of hearing it), but he said he was
quite ignorant of having it in his possession.
When Harry argued with him, Burnett sent
for his batman and cursed him for taking
another officer's property. The wretched man
mumbled that he had 'found' it, and with-
drew ; and we all sat in a silence teeming with
distrustful thoughts. We were sorry for the
batman ; we were sorry for Harry. Burnett
may not have taken the mess-tin with his own
hands, but morally he stood convicted of an
action which was 'dirty.'

Then Burnett and Harry took a working-
party together to dig in the gully. Burnett was
the senior officer, but left Harry to work all
night in the whispering rain of stray bullets,

while he sat in an Engineers' dug-out and drank whisky. Harry did not object to this, the absence of Burnett being always congenial to him. But next day there came a complimentary message from the Brigadier about the work of that working-party. Burnett was sent for and warmly praised by the Colonel. Burnett stood smugly and said nothing. Harry, when he heard of it, was furious, and wanted, he said, to ' have a row ' with him. What he expected Burnett to say, I don't know ; the man could hardly stand before his Colonel and say, ' Sir, Penrose did all the work, I was in the Engineers' dug-out nearly all the time with my friends, and had one or two drinks.' A row, in any case, would be intolerable in that cramped, intimate existence, and I dissuaded Harry, though I made Egerton have a few words with Burnett on the subject. Harry contented himself with ironic comments on Burnett's ' gallantry ' and ' industry ', asking him blandly at meals if he expected to get his promotion over that working-party, and suggesting to Egerton that Burnett should take Harry's next turn of duty ' because he is so good at it.' This made Burnett beautifully angry. But it was bitter badinage, and did not improve the atmosphere.

There were a number of such incidents between the two ; they were very petty in

themselves, some of them, like flies, but in their
cumulative effect very large and distressing.
In many cases there was no verbal engagement,
or only an angry, inarticulate mutter.   Public,
unfettered angers were necessarily avoided.
But this pent-up, suppressed condition of the
quarrel made it more malignant, like a disease.
And it got on Harry's nerves ; indeed, it got
on mine.   It became an active element in that
complex irritation which was eating into his
young system ; it was leagued with the flies,
and the dust, and the smells, and the bad food,
and the wind, and the harassing shells of the
Turks, and the disgustful torment of disease.

III

For Harry was a very sick man.   He had
endured through all the stages of dysentery
and now lived with that awful legacy of weakness of which I have spoken.   And the disease
had not wholly left him, for some days he
lay faint with excruciating spasms of pain.
Slightly built and constitutionally fragile at
the beginning, he was now a mere wasted wisp
of a man.   The flesh seemed to have melted
from his face, and when he stood naked on the
beach it seemed that the moving of his bone
must soon tear holes in the unsubstantial skin.
Standing in the trench with the two points of

his collar-bone jutting out like promontories above his shirt, and a pale film of dust over his face, he looked like the wan ghost of some forgotten soldier.   On the Western Front, where one case of dysentery created a panic among the authorities, and in the most urgent days they have never had to rely on skeletons to fight, he would long since have been bundled off. But in this orgy of disease no officer could be sent away who was willing to stay and could still totter up the gully.   And Harry would not go.   When he went to the battalion doctor it was with an airy request for the impotent palliatives then provided for early dysentery, and with no suggestion of the soul-destroying sickness that was upon him.   One day he would not come down to the rocks and bathe, so feeble he was.   'I know now,' he said, 'the meaning of that bit in the Psalms, " My knees are like water and all my bones are out of joint." '   'Harry,' I said, 'you 're not fit to stay here—why not go sick ? '   At which he smiled weakly, and said that he might be better in a day or two.   Pathetic hope ! all men had it.   And so Hewett and I walked down, a little sadly, alone, marvelling at the boy's courage. For it seemed to us that he wanted to stay and see it through, and if indeed he might recover we could not afford to lose him.   So we said no more.

But by degrees I gained a different impression. Harry still opened his mind to Hewett and myself more than to any one else, but it was by no direct speech, rather by the things he did not say, the sentences half finished, the look in his eyes, that the knowledge came— that Harry did want to go away. The romantic impulse had perished long since in that ruined trench ; but now even the more mundane zest of doing his duty had lost its savour in the long ordeal of sickness and physical distress. He did want to go sick. He had only to speak a word ; and still he would not go. When I knew this, I marvelled at his courage yet more.

For many days I watched him fighting this lonely conflict with himself, a conflict more terrible and exacting than any battle. Sometimes the doctor came and sat under our olive-tree, and some of us spoke jestingly of the universal sickness, and asked him how ill we must be before he would send us home. Harry alone sat silent ; it was no joke to him. ' And how do *you* feel now, Penrose ? ' said the doctor. ' Are you getting your arrowroot all right ? ' Harry opened his mouth—but for a moment said nothing. I think it had been in his mind to say what he did feel, but he only murmured, ' All right, thank you, doctor.' The doctor looked at him queerly. He knew well enough, but it was his task to keep men on the Peninsula, not to send them away.

Once I spent an afternoon in one of the hospital ships in the bay. When I came back and told them of the cool wards and pleasant nurses, and all the peace and cleanliness and comfort that was there, I caught Harry's wistful gaze upon me, and I stopped. It was well enough for the rest of us in comparative health to imagine luxuriously those unattainable amenities. None of us were ill enough then to go sick if we wished it. Harry was. And I knew that such talk must be an intolerable temptation.

Then one day, on his way up to the line with a working-party, he nearly fainted. ' I felt it coming on,' he told me, ' in a block. I thought to myself, " This is the end of it all for me, anyhow." I actually did go off for a moment, I think, and then some one pushed me from behind—and as we moved on it wore off again. I did swear——' Harry stopped, realizing the confession he had made. I tried to feel for myself the awful bitterness of that awakening in the stifling trench, shuffling uphill with the flies. . . . But he had told me now everything I had only guessed before, and once more I urged him to go sick and have done with it.

' I would,' he said, ' only I 'm not sure . . .

I know I'm jolly ill, and not fit for a thing
. . . but I'm not sure if it's only that. . . .
I was pretty brave when I got here, I think'
(I nodded), ' and I think I am still . . . but
last time we were in the line I found I didn't
like looking over the top nearly so much . . .
so I want to be sure that I'm quite all right
. . . in that way . . . before I go sick. . . .
Besides, you know what everybody says. . . .'

' Nobody could say anything about you,' I
told him ; ' one's only got to look at you to
see that you've got one foot in the grave.'
' Well, we go up again to-morrow,' he said,
' and if I'm not better after that, I'll think
about it again.'

I had to be content with that, though I
was not content. For my fears were fulfilled,
since in the grip of this sickness he had begun
at last to be doubtful of his own courage.

But that night Burnett went to the doctor
and said that he was too ill to go on. So far
as the rest of us knew, he had never had anything but the inevitable preliminary attack
of dysentery, though it is only fair to say that
most of us were so wrapped up in the exquisite
contemplation of our own sufferings, that we
had little time to study the condition of others.
The doctor, however, had no doubts about
Burnett ; he sent him back to us with a flea
in his ear and a dose of chlorodyne. The

story leaked out quickly, and there was much comment adverse to Burnett. When Harry heard it, he led me away to his dug-out. It was an evening of heavy calm, like the inside of a cathedral. Only a few mules circling dustily at exercise in the velvet gloom, and the distant glimmer of the Scotsmen's fires, made any stir of movement. The men had gone early to their blankets, and now sang softly their most sentimental songs, reserved always for the night before another journey to the line. They sang them in a low croon of ecstatic melancholy, marvellously in tune with the purple hush of the evening. For all its aching regret it was a sound full of hope and gentle resolution. Harry whispered to me, ' You heard about Burnett ? Thank God, nobody can say those things about me ! I 'm not going off this Peninsula till I 'm pushed off.'

I said nothing. It was a heroic sentiment, and this was the heroic hour. It is what men say in the morning that matters.

In the morning we moved off as the sun came up. There had been heavy firing nearly all night, and over Achi Baba in the cloudless sky there hung a portent. It was as though some giant had been blowing smoke-rings, and with inhuman dexterity had twined and laced these rings together, without any of them losing their perfection of form. . . . As the sun came up these cloud-rings stood out a rosy pink against the blue distance, and while we marched through, the sleeping camps turned gently through dull gold to pale pearl. I have never known what made this marvel, a few clouds forgotten by the wind, or the smoke of the night's battle ; but I marched with my eyes upon it all the stumbling way to Achi Baba. And when I found Harry at a halt, he, too, was gazing at the wonder with all his men. ' It 's an omen ', he said.

' Good or bad ? '

' Good,' he said.

I have never understood omens ; I suppose they are good or bad according to the mind of the man who sees them : and I was glad that Harry thought it was good.

VI

IT was one of the Great Dates: one of those red dates which build up the calendar of a soldier's past, and dwell in his memory when the date of his own birth is almost forgotten. It is strange what definite sign-posts these dates of a man's battle-days become in his calculation of time—like the foundation of Rome. An old soldier will sigh and say, ' Yes I know that was when Jim died—it was ten days after the Fourth of June,' or, ' I was promoted the day before the Twelfth of July.'

The years pile up, and zero after zero day is added for ever to his primitive calendar, and not one of them is thrust from his reverent memory ; but at each anniversary he wakes and says, ' This is the 3rd of February, or the 1st of July,' and thinks of old companions who went down on that day ; and though he has seen glorious successes since, he will ever think with a special tenderness of the black early failures when he first saw battle and his friends going under. And if in any place where soldiers gather and tell old tales there are two men who can say to each other, ' I, too, was at Helles on such a date,' there is a great bond between them.

On one of these days we sat under the olive-tree and waited. Up the hill one of that long series of heroic, costly, semi-successes was going through. We were in reserve. We had done six turns in the trenches without doing an attack. When we came out we were very ready to attack, very sure of ourselves. Now we were not so sure of ourselves; we were waiting, and there was a terrible noise. Very early the guns had begun, and everywhere, from the Straits to the sea, were the sharp barkings of the French 'seventy-fives,' thinly assisted by the British artillery, which was scanty and had almost no ammunition. But the big ships came out from Imbros and stood off and swelled the tumult, dropping their huge shells on the very peak of the little sugar-loaf that tops Achi Baba, and covering his western slopes with monstrous eruptions of black and yellow.

Down in the thirsty wilderness of the rest-camps the few troops in reserve lay restless under occasional olive-trees, or huddled under the exiguous shelter of ground-sheets stretched over their scratchings in the earth. They looked up and saw the whole of the great hill swathed in smoke and dust and filthy fumes, and heard the ruthless crackle of the Turks' rifles, incredibly rapid and sustained; and they thought of their friends scrambling over in the bright sun, trying to get to those rifles. They themselves were thin and wasted with disease, and this uncertainty of waiting in readiness for they knew not what plucked at their nerves.   They could not rest or sleep, for the flies crawled over their mouths and eyes and tormented them ceaselessly, and great storms of dust swept upon them as they lay. They were parched with thirst, but they must not drink, for their water-bottles were filled with the day's allowance, and none knew when they would be filled again.   If a man took out of his haversack a chunk of bread, it was immediately black with flies, and he could not eat.   Sometimes a shell came over the Straits from Asia with a quick, shrill shriek, and burst at the top of the cliffs near the staff officers who stood there and gazed up the hill with glasses. All morning the noise increased, and the shells streamed up the hill with a sound like a hundred expresses vanishing into a hundred tunnels : and there was no news.   But soon the wounded began to trickle down, and there were rumours of a great success with terrible losses.   In the afternoon the news became uncertain and disturbing.   Most of the morning's fruits had been lost.   And by evening they knew that indeed it had been a terrible day.

Under our olive-tree we were very fidgety. There had been no mail for many days, and we

had only month-old copies of the *Mail* and the
Weekly Times, which we pretended listlessly to
read. Eustace had an ancient *Nation*, and
Hewett a shilling edition of *Vanity Fair*. Harry
in the morning kept climbing excitedly up the
trees to gaze at the obscure haze of smoke on
the hill, and trying vainly to divine what was
going on ; but after a little he too sat silent
and brooding. We were no longer irritable
with each other, but studiously considerate, as
if each felt that to-morrow he might want to
take back a spiteful word and the other be
dead.   All our valises and our sparse mess
furniture had long been packed away, for we
had now been standing by for twenty-four
hours, and we lay uneasily on the hard ground
shifting continually from posture to posture to
escape the unfriendly protuberances of the soil.
In the tree the crickets chirped on always, in
strange indifference to the storm of noise about
them.   They were hateful, those crickets.

Now and then Egerton was summoned to
Headquarters ; and when he came back each
man said to himself, ' He has got our orders.'
And some would not look at him, but talked
suddenly of something else.   And some said to
him with a painful cheeriness, ' Any orders ? '
and when he shook his head, cursed a little but
in their hearts wondered if they were glad.
For the waiting was bad indeed, but who knew

what tasks they would have when the orders came ! . . . Often the Reserves had the worst of it in these affairs . . . a forlorn hope of an attack without artillery . . . digging a new line under fire . . . beating off the counter-attack. . . .

But the waiting became intolerable, and all were glad, an hour before sunset, when we filed off slowly by half-platoons. Every gun was busy again, and all along the path to the hill, batteries of 'seventy-fives' barked suddenly from unsuspected holes, so close that a man's heart seemed to halt at the shock. The gully was full of confusion and wounded, and tired officers and odd groups of men bandying rumours and arguing in the sun. Halfway up the tale came mysteriously down the line that we were to attack a trench by ourselves ; a whole brigade had tried and failed—there was a redoubt—there were endless machine-guns. . . . Some laughed—' a rumour ' ; but most men felt in their hearts that there was something in it, and inwardly ' pulled themselves together.' At last they were to be in a real battle, and walk naked in the open through the rapid fire. And as they moved on, there came over them an overpowering sense of the irrevocable. They thought of that summer day in 1914 when they walked light-hearted into the recruiting office. It had seemed a small thing then, but that was what had done it, had brought them into this blazing gully, with the frogs croaking, and the men moaning in corners with their legs messed up. . . . If they had known about this gully then and these flies, and this battle they were going to, then, perhaps, they would have done something else in that August . . . gone into a dockyard . . . joined the A.S.C. like Jim Roberts. . . . Well, they hadn't, and they were not really sorry . . . only let there be no more waiting . . . and let it be quick and merciful, no stomach wounds and nastiness . . . no lying out in the scrub for a day with the sun, and the flies, and no water.

Look at that officer on the stretcher . . . *he* won't last long . . . remember his face . . . his platoon relieved us somewhere . . . where was it ? . . . Hope I don't get one like him . . . nasty mess . . . would like one in the shoulder if it's got to be . . . hospital ship . . . get home, perhaps . . . no, they send you to Egypt . . . officer said so. . . . Hallo, halting here . . . Merton trench . . . old Reserve Line. . . . Getting dark . . . night-attack ? . . . not wait till dawn, I hope . . . can't stand much more waiting. . . . Pass the word, Company Commanders to see the Colonel . . . that's done it, there goes Egerton . . . good man, thinks a lot of me . . . try not to let him down. . . .

But what Egerton and the others heard from the Colonel made a vain thing of all this bracing of men's spirits. There was a muddle ; the attack was cancelled . . . no one knew where the Turks were, where anybody was . . . we were to stay the night in this old reserve trench and relieve the front line in the morning. . . .

When Egerton told his officers only Burnett spoke : he said ' Damn. *As* usual. I wanted a go at the old Turk ' : and we knew that it was not true. The rest of us said nothing, for we were wondering if it were true of ourselves. I went with Harry to his platoon ; they too said nothing, and their faces were expression-less. But they were cold now, and hungry, and suddenly very tired ; and they had no real fire of battle in them ; they had waited too long for this crowning experience of an attack, braced themselves for it too often to be disappointed ; and I knew that they were glad. But they did not mind being glad ; they pondered no doubts about themselves, only curled up like animals in corners to sleep.

Harry, too, no doubt, had braced himself like the rest of us, and he, too, must have been glad, glad to lie down and look forward after all to seeing another sunrise. But I thought of his doubts about himself, and I felt that this business was far from easing his burden. For me and for the men it was a simple thing—the postponement of a battle with the Turks ; for Harry it was the postponement of a personal test : the battle inside him still went on ; only it went on more bitterly.

II

There was a great muddle in front. Troops of two different brigades were hopelessly entangled in the shallow trenches they had taken from the Turks. They had few officers left, and their staffs had the most imperfect impressions of the whereabouts of their mangled commands. So the sun was well up when we finally took over the line ; this was in defiance of all tradition, but the Turk was shaken and did not molest us. The men who passed us on their way down grimly wished us joy of what they had left ; their faces were pale and drawn, full of loathing and weariness, but they said little ; and the impression grew that there was something up there which they could not even begin to describe. It was a still, scorching morning, and as we moved on the air became heavy with a sickening stench, the most awful of all smells that man can be called to endure, because it preyed on the imagination as well as the senses. For we knew now what it was. We came into a Turkish trench, broad

and shallow.   In the first bay lay two bodies—
a Lowlander and a Turk.   They lay where they
had killed each other, and they were very foul
and loathsome in the sun.   A man looked up
at them and passed on, thinking, ' Glad I
haven't got to stay here.'   In the next bay
there were three dead, all Englishmen ; and in
the next there were more—and he thought, ' It
was a hot fight just here.'   But as he moved on,
and in each succeeding bay beheld the same
corrupt aftermath of yesterday's battle, the
suspicion came to him that this was no local
horror.   Over the whole front of the attack,
along two lines of trenches, these regiments of
dead were everywhere found, strung in unnatural
heaps along the parapets, or sprawling horribly
half into the trench so that he touched them
as he passed.   Yet still he could not believe,
and at each corner thought, ' Surely there will
be none in this bay.'

But always there were more ; until, if he were
not careful or very callous, it began to get on
his nerves, so that at the traverses he almost
prayed that there might be no more beyond.
Yet many did not realize what was before them
till they were finally posted in the bays they
were to garrison—three or four in a bay.   Then
they looked up at the sprawling horrors on the
parapet and behind them, just above their
heads, and knew that these were to be their

close companions all that sweltering day, and
perhaps beyond.   The regiment we had relieved
had been too exhausted by the attack, or too
short-handed, to bury more than a few, and the
Turkish snipers made it impossible to do anything during the day.   And so we sat all the
scorching hours of the sun, or moved listlessly
up and down, trying not to look upwards. . . .
But there was a hideous fascination about the
things, so that after a few hours a man came to
know the bodies in his bay with a sickening
intimacy, and could have told you many details
about each of them—their regiment, and how
they lay, and how they had died, and little
things about their uniforms, a missing button,
or some papers, or an old photograph sticking
out of a pocket. . . . All of them were alive
with flies, and at noon when we took out our
bread and began to eat, these flies rose in a great
black swarm and fell upon the food in our hands.
After that no one could eat.   All day men were
being sent away by the doctor, stricken with
sheer nausea by the flies and the stench and the
things they saw, and went retching down the
trench.   To keep away the awful reek we went
about for a little in the old gas-helmets, but
the heat and burden of them in the hot, airless
trench was intolerable.   The officers had no
dug-outs, but sat under the parapets like the
men.   No officer went sick ; no officer could

be spared ; and indeed we seemed to have a greater power of resistance to this ordeal of disgust than the men. But I don't know how Harry survived it. Being already in a very bad way physically, it affected him more than the rest of us, and it was the first day I had seen his cheerfulness defeated. At the worst he had always been ready to laugh a little at our misfortunes, the great safety-valve of a soldier, and make ironical remarks about Burnett or the Staff. This day he had no laugh left in him, and I thought sadly of that first evening when he jumped over the parapet to look at a dead Turk. He had seen enough now.

In the evening the Turk was still a little chastened, and all night we laboured at the burying of the bodies. It was bad work, but so strong was the horror upon us that every man who could be spared took his part, careless of sleep or rest, so long as he should not sit for another day with those things. But we could only bury half of them that night and all the next day we went again through that lingering torment. And in the afternoon when we had orders to go up to the front line after dusk for an attack we were glad. It was one of the very few moments in my experience when the war-correspondent's legend of a regiment's pleasure at the prospect of battle came true. For anything was welcome if only we could get out of that trench, away from the smell and the flies, away from those bodies.

I am not going to tell you all about that attack, only so much of it as affects this history, which is the history of a man and not of the war.   It was a one-battalion affair, and eventually a failure.   D Company was in reserve, and our only immediate task was to provide a small digging-party, forty men under an officer, to dig some sort of communication ditch to the new line when taken.   Burnett was told off for this job ; we took these things more or less in turn, and it was his turn.   And Burnett did not like it.   We sat round a single candle under a waterproof sheet in a sort of open recess at the back of the front line, while Egerton gave him his orders.   And there ran in my head the old bit about ' they all began with one accord to make excuse.'   Burnett made no actual excuse ; he could not.   But he asked aggressive questions about the arrangements which plainly said that he considered this task too dangerous and too difficult for Burnett.   He wanted more men, he wanted another officer—but no more could be spared from an already small reserve. He was full of ' the high ground on the right ' from which his party would ' obviously ' be

enfiladed and shot down to a man.   However,
he went.   And we sat listening to the rapid fire
or the dull thud of bombs, until in front a
strange quiet fell, but to right and left were the
sounds of many machine-guns.   As usual, no
one knew what had happened, but we expected
a summons at any moment.   We were all
restless and jumpy, particularly Harry.   For
a man who has doubts of himself or too much
imagination, to be in reserve is the worst thing
possible.   Harry was talkative again, and held
forth about the absurdity of the whole attack,
as to which he was perfectly right.   But I felt
that all the time he was thinking, ' Shall I do
the right thing ?   Shall I do the right thing ?
Shall I make a mess of it ? '

I went out and looked over the parapet, but
could make nothing out.   Then I saw two
figures loom through the dark and scramble
into the trench.   And after them came others
all along the line, coming in anyhow, in disorder.
Then Burnett came along the trench, and
crawled in under the waterproof sheet.   I
followed.   ' It 's no good,' he was saying,
' the men won't stick it.   It 's just what I told
you . . . enfiladed from that high ground over
there—two machine-guns. . . .'

' How many casualties have you had ? ' said
Egerton.

' One killed and two wounded.'

There was silence, but it was charged with eloquent thoughts. It was clear what had happened. The machine-guns were firing blindly from the right, probably over the heads of the party. The small casualties showed that. Casualties are the test. No doubt the men had not liked the stream of bullets overhead ; at any moment the gun might lower. But there was nothing to prevent the digging being done, given an officer who would assert himself and keep the men together. That was what an officer was for. And Burnett had failed. He had let the company down.

Egerton, I knew, was considering what to do. The job had to be done. But should he send Burnett again, with orders not to return until he had finished, as he deserved, or should he send a more reliable officer and make sure ?

Then Harry burst in : ' Let me take my platoon,' he said, ' they 'll stick it all right.' And his tone was full of contempt for Burnett, full of determination. No doubts about him now.

Well, we sent him out with his platoon. And all night they dug and sweated in the dark. The machine-gun did lower at times, and there were many casualties, but Harry moved up and down in the open, cheerful and encouraging, getting away the wounded, and there were no

signs of the men not sticking it. I went out
and stayed with him for an hour or so, and
thought him wonderful. Curious from what
strange springs inspiration comes. For Harry,
for the second time, had been genuinely inspired
by the evil example of his enemy. Probably,
in the first place, he had welcomed the chance
of doing something at last, of putting his doubts
to the test, but I am sure that what chiefly
carried him through that night, weak and
exhausted as he was, was the thought, ' Burnett
let them down ; Burnett let them down ; I 'm
not going to let them down.' Anyhow he did
very well.

But in the morning he was carried down to
the beach in a high fever. And perhaps it was
just as well, for I think Burnett would have
done him a mischief.

VII

SO Harry stayed till he was 'pushed' off, as he had promised. And I was glad he had gone like that. I had long wanted him to leave the Peninsula somehow, for I felt he should be spared for greater things, but, knowing something of his peculiar temperament, I did not want his career there to end on a note of simple failure—a dull surrender to sickness in the rest-camp. As it turned out, the accident of the digging-party, and the way in which Harry had seized his chance, sent him off with a renewed confidence in himself and, with regard to Burnett, even a sense of triumph. So I was not surprised when his letters began to reveal something of the old enthusiastic Harry, chafing at the dreary routine of the Depot, and looking for adventure again. But I am anticipating.

They sent him home, of course. It was no good keeping any one in his condition at Egypt or Malta, for the prolonged dysentery had produced the usual complications. I had a letter from Malta, and one from the Mediterranean Club at Gibraltar, where he had a sultry week looking over the bay, seeing the ships steam out for England, he told me, and longing to be in one. For it took many months to wash away the taste of the Peninsula, and much more than the austere comforts of the hospital at Gibraltar. Even the hot August sun in the Alameda was hatefully reminiscent. Then six weeks' milk diet at a hospital in Devonshire, convalescence, and a month's leave.

Then Harry married a wife. I did not know the lady—a Miss Thickness—and she does not come into the story very much, though she probably affected it a good deal. Wives usually do affect a soldier's story, though they are one of the many things which by the absolute official standard of military duty are necessarily not reckoned with at all. Not being the president of a court-martial I did reckon with it ; and when I had read Harry's letter about his wedding I said : ' We shan't see *him* again.' For in those early years it was generally assumed that a man returned from service at the front need not go out again (unless he wished) for a period almost incalculably prolonged. And, being a newly married man myself, I had no reason to suppose that Harry would want to rush into the breach just yet.

But about May—that would be 1916 ; we had done with Gallipoli and come to France, after four months' idling in the Aegean Islands —I had another letter, much delayed, from which I will give you an extract :

' *I never thought I should want to go out again*

*(you remember we all swore we never should), but
I do.   I'm fed to the teeth with this place* (the
Depot, in Dorsetshire) ; *nothing but company
drill and lectures on march discipline, and all the
old stuff.   We still attack Hill 219 twice weekly
in exactly the same way, and still no one but a few
of the officers knows exactly which hill it is, since
we always stop halfway for lunch-time, or because
there's hopeless confusion. . . . There's nobody
amusing here.   Williams has got a company and
swanks like blazes about ' the front,' but I think
most people see through him. . . . My wife's
got rooms in a cottage near here, but they won't let
me sleep out, and I don't get there till pretty late
most days. . . . Can't you get the Colonel to
apply for me ?   I don't believe it's allowed, but
he's sure to be able to wangle it.   Otherwise I shall
be here for the rest of the war, because the more
you've been out the less likely you are to get out
again, if you want to, while there are lots who
don't want to go, and wouldn't be any earthly good,
and stand in hourly danger of being sent. . . .
I want to see France. . . .'*

I answered on a single sheet :

' *All very well, but what about Mrs. P. ?   Does
she concur ?* '   (I told you I was a married
man.)

His answer was equally brief :

' *She doesn't know, but she would.*'

Well, it wasn't my business, so we ' wangled '

it (I was adjutant then), and Harry came out to
France.   But I was sorry for Mrs. Penrose.

II

I do not know if all this seems tedious and
unnecessary ; I hope not, for it is very relevant
to the end of the story, and if this record had
been in the hands of certain persons the end of
the story might have been different.   I do not
know.   Certainly it ought to have been different.

Anyhow, Harry came to France and found
us in the line at Souchez.   The recuperative
power of the young soldier is marvellous.   No
one but myself would have said that this was
not the same Harry of a year ago ; for he was
fit and fresh and bubbling over with keenness.
Only myself, who had sat over the Dardanelles
with him and talked about Troy, knew what
was missing.   There were no more romantic
illusions about war, and, I think, no more
military ambitions.   Only he was sufficiently
rested to be very keen again, and had not yet
seen enough of it to be ordinarily bored.

And in that summer of 1916 there was much
to be said for life in the Souchez sector.   It was
a ' peace-time ' sector, where divisions stayed
for months at a time, and one went in and out
like clockwork at ritual intervals, each time
into the same trenches, the same deep dug-outs,

each time back to the same billets, or the same huts in the same wood. All the deserted fields about the line were a mass of poppies and corn-flowers, and they hung over one in extravagant masses as one walked up the communication trench. In the thick woods round Bouvigny and Noulette there were clusters of huts where the resting-time was very warm and lazy and companionable, with much white wine and singing in the evenings. Or one took a horse and rode into Coupigny or Barlin where there had not been too much war, but one could dine happily at the best estaminet, and then ride back contentedly under the stars.

In the line also there was not too much war. Few of the infantry on either side ever fired their rifles ; and only a few bombers with rifle grenades tried to injure the enemy. There were short sectors of the line on either side which became spasmodically dangerous because of these things, and at a fixed hour each day the Germans blew the same portions of the line to dust with minenwerfers, our men having departed elsewhere half an hour previously, according to the established routine from which neither side ever diverged. Our guns were very busy by spasms, and every day destroyed small sections of the thick red masses of the German wire, which were every night religiously repaired. The German guns were very few, for the Somme battle was raging, but at times they flung whizz-bangs vaguely about the line or dropped big shells on the great brows of the Lorette Heights behind us. From the high ground we held there was a good view, with woods and red and white villages on the far hills beyond the Germans ; and away to the left one looked over the battered pit country towards Lens, with the tall pit-towers everywhere, all crumpled and bent into uncouth shapes, and grey slag-heaps rising like the Pyramids out of a wilderness of broken red cottages. To the south-east began the Vimy Ridge, where the red Pimple frowned over the lines at the Lorette Heights and all day there was the foam and blackness of bursting shells.

In the night there was much patrolling and bursts of machine-gun fire, and a few snipers, and enormous labours at the 'improvement of the line,' wiring and revetting, and exquisite work with sand-bags.

It was all very gentle and friendly and artificial, and we were happy together.

Burnett had left us, on some detached duty or other, and in that gentler atmosphere Eustace was a good companion again.

Men grew lusty and well, and one could have continued there indefinitely without much injury to body or mind. But sometimes on a clear night we saw all the southern sky afire

from some new madness on the Somme, and
knew that somewhere in France there was real
war. The correspondents wrote home that
the regiments ' condemned so long to the
deadening inactivity of trench warfare were
longing only for their turn at the Great Battle.'
No doubt they had authority : though I never
met one of those regiments. For our part we
were happy where we were. We had had
enough for the present.

III

But I digress. And yet—no. For I want
you to keep this idea of the diversity of war
conditions before you, and how a man may be
in a fighting unit for many months and yet go
unscathed even in spirit. Or in the most
Arcadian parts of the battle area he may come
alone against some peculiar shock from which
he never recovers. It is all chance.

We made Harry scout officer again, and he
was very keen. Between us and the German
lines was a honeycomb of old disused trenches
where French and Germans had fought for
many months before they sat down to watch
each other across this maze. They were all
overgrown now with flowers and thick grasses,
but for the purposes of future operations it
was important to know all about them, and

every night Harry wriggled out and dropped
into one of these to creep and explore, and
afterwards put them on the map.   Sometimes
I went a little way with him, and I did not like
it.   It was very creepy in those forgotten alleys,
worse than crawling outside in the open, I
think, because of the intense blackness and the
infinite possibilities of ambush.

The Boches, we knew, were playing the same
game as ourselves, and might always be round
the next traverse, so that every ten yards one
went through a new ordeal of expectancy and
stealthy, strained investigation.   One stood
breathless at the corner, listening, peering,
quivering with the strain of it, and then a rat
dropped into the next ' bay,' or behind us one
of our Lewis guns blazed off a few bursts,
shattering the silence.   Surely there was some
one near moving hurriedly under cover of the
noise !   Then you stood again, stiff and cramped
with the stillness, and you wanted insanely to
cough, or shift your weight on to the other foot,
your nose itched and the grasses tickled your
ear—but you must not stir, must hardly breathe.
For now all the lines have become mysteriously
hushed, and no man fires ; far away one can
hear the rumble of the German limbers coming
up with rations to the dump, and the quiet
becomes unbearable, so that you long for some
Titanic explosion to break it and set you free

from waiting. Then a machine-gun opens
again, and you slip round the corner to find—
nothing at all, only more blackness and the rats
scuttling away into the grass, and perhaps the
bones of a Frenchman. And then you begin
all over again. . . . When he has done this
sort of thing many times without any happening, an imperfect scout becomes careless through
sheer weariness, and begins to blunder noisily
ahead. And sooner or later he goes under.
But Harry was a natural scout, well trained, and
from first to last kept the same care, the same
admirable patience, and this means a great
strain on body and mind. . . . In those old
trenches you could go right up to the German
line, two hundred yards away, and this Harry
often did. The Germans had small posts at
these points, waiting, and were very ready with
bombs and rifle grenades. It was a poor look-
out if you were heard about there, and perhaps
badly wounded, so that you could not move,
two hundred yards away from friends and all
those happy soldiers who spent their nights
comfortably in trenches when you were out
there on your stomach. Perhaps your companion would get away and bring help. Or he
too might be hit or killed, and then you would
lie there for days and nights, alone in a dark
hole, with the rats scampering and smelling
about you, till you died of starvation or loss of

blood. You would lie there listening to your
own men chattering in the distance at their
wiring, and neither they nor any one would
find you or know where you were, till months
hence some other venturesome scout stumbled
on your revolver in the dark. Or maybe the
line would advance at last, and some salvage
party come upon your uniform rotting in the
ditch, and they would take off your identity
disc and send it in to Head-quarters, and shovel
a little earth above your bones. It might be
many years.

I am not an imaginative man, but that was
the kind of thought I had while I prowled
round with Harry (and I never went so far as
he). He even had an occasional jest at the
Germans, and once planted an old dummy close
up to their lines. There was stony ground
there, and, as they took it there, he told me, it
clattered. The next night he went there again
in case the Germans came out to capture
' Reggie.' They did not, but every evening
for many months they put a barrage of rifle-
grenades all about that dummy.

Then there was much talk of ' raids,' and all
the opposite wire had to be patrolled and
examined for gaps and weak places. This
meant crawling in the open close up to the
enemy, naked under the white flares ; and sometimes they fell to earth within a few feet of a

scout and sizzled brilliantly for interminable seconds ; there was a sniper somewhere near, and perhaps a machine-gun section, and surely they could see him, so large, so illuminated, so monstrously visible he felt. It was easy when there was not too much quiet, but many echoes of scattered shots and the noise of bullets rocketing into space, or long bursts of machine-gun fire, to cover your movements. But when that terrible silence fell it was very difficult. For then how loud was the rustle of your stealthiest wriggle, how sinister the tiny sounds of insects in the grass. Everywhere there were stray strands of old barbed wire which caught in your clothes and needed infinite patience to disentangle ; when you got rid of one barb another clung to you as the wire sprang back or, if you were not skilful, it clashed on a post or a rifle, or a tin can, with a noise like cymbals. You came across strange things as you crawled out there—dead bodies, and bits of equipment, and huge unexploded shells. Or you touched a rat or a grass-snake that made you shiver as it moved ; the rats and the field-mice ran over you if you lay still for long, and once Harry saw a German patrol-dog sniffing busily in front of him. Sometimes as you went up wind you put your hand suddenly on a dead man, and had to lie close beside him for cover. Or you scented him far off like a dog nosing through the grass, and made him a landmark whispering to your companion, ' Keep fifty yards from the dead 'un,' or ' Make for the dead Boche.'

When the lights went up you lay very close, peering ahead under your cap ; and as they fell away to the ground all your vision became full of moving things and fugitive shadows. The thick rows of wiring posts looked like men working, and that cluster of stone like the head of a man in a shell-hole, watching . . . watching you . . . gone in an instant. . . . Then you waited tensely for the next light. There is the murmur of voices somewhere, very difficult to locate. For a long while you stalk it, ready to attack some patrol, some working-party. Then you hear a familiar Tyneside curse . . . it is A Company wiring, with much noise.

All this, as I have said, is a heavy strain on mind and body and nerve. It requires a peculiar kind of courage, a lonely, cold-blooded kind of courage. Many men who would do well in a slap-dash fight in the light of day are useless as scouts. Not only are they noisy and impatient, but they cannot stand it.

And yet it is no job for a very imaginative man. There are too many things you can imagine, if you once begin. The more you know about it, the more there is to imagine, and the greater the strain becomes. Now

Harry had a very vivid imagination, and he knew all about it—and yet he played the game nearly every night we were in the line for three months . . . nothing theatrical, you understand, nor even heroic by popular standards, no stabbing affrays, no medals . . . but by my standards it *was* very nearly heroic, and I don't know how he did it.

But this was forgotten later on.

IV

Then Harry had a shock. There was a large sap running out from our line along the crown of a steep ridge. This sap was not held during the day, but at night was peopled with bombers and snipers, and it was a great starting-place for the patrols. One night Harry went out from this sap and crawled down the face of the ridge. It was a dark night, and the Boches were throwing up many flares. One of these came to earth ten yards from Harry. At that moment he was halfway down the slope, crouched on one knee. However, when flares are about, to keep still in any posture is better than to move, so Harry remained rigid. But one of the new scouts behind was just leaving the sap, and hovered uncertainly on the skyline as the light flared and sizzled below. Possibly he was seen, possibly what followed was a chance freak of the Germans. Anyhow, a moment later they opened with every machine-gun in the line, with rifles, rifle-grenades, and high-velocity shells. So venomous was the fire that every man in the line believed—and afterwards hotly asserted —that the whole fury of it was concentrated on his particular yard of trench. Few of us thought of the unhappy scouts lying naked outside. Harry, of course, flattened himself to the ground, and tried to wriggle into a hollow ; on level ground you may with luck be safe under wild fire of this kind for a long time. Being on a slope, Harry was hopelessly exposed. ' I lay there,' he told me, ' and simply sweated with funk; you won't believe me, but at one time I could literally *feel* a stream of machine-gun bullets ruffling my hair, and thudding into the bank just above my back . . . and they dropped half a dozen whizz-bangs just in front of me. While it was going on I couldn't have moved for a thousand pounds. . . . I felt *pinned* to the ground . . . then there was a lull, and I leapt up . . . so did old Smith . . . bolted for the sap, and simply dived in head first . . . they were still blazing off sixteen to the dozen, and it was the mercy of God we weren't hit . . . talk about wind-up. . . . And when we got in two bombers thought it was an attack, and took us for Boches. . . . Rather

funny, while the strafe was going on I kept
thinking, " Poor old Smith, he 's a married
man " (he was a few yards from me) . . . and
Smith tells me *he* was thinking, " Mr. Penrose
. . . a married man . . . married man." . . .
What about some more whisky ? '

Well, he made a joke of it, as one tries to do
as long as possible, and that night was almost
happily exhilarated, as a man sometimes is
after escaping narrowly from an adventure.
But I could see that it had been a severe shock.
The next night he had a cold and a bad cough,
and said he would not go out for fear of ' making
a noise and giving the show away.' The
following night he went out, but came in very
soon, and sat rather glum in the dug-out,
thinking of something. (I always waited up
till he came in to report, and we used to ' dis-
cuss the situation ' over some whisky or a little
white wine.)

The following day the Colonel gave him a
special job to do. There was the usual talk
of a ' raid ' on a certain section of the enemy
lines ; but there was a theory that this particular section had been evacuated. Flares
were sent up from all parts of it, but this was
supposed to be the work of one man, a hard
worker, who walked steadily up and down,
pretending to be a company. Harry was told
off to test the truth of this myth—to get right

up to that trench, to look in, and see what was in it. It was a thing he had done twice before, at least, though myself I should not have cared to do it at all. It meant the usual breathless, toilsome wriggle across No Man's Land, avoiding the flares and the two snipers who covered that bit of ground, finding a gap in the wire, getting through without being seen, without noise, without catching his clothes on a wandering barb, or banging his revolver against a multitude of tin cans. Then you had to listen and wait, and, if possible, get a look into the trench. When (and if) you had done that you had to get back, turn round in a tiny space, pass the same obstacles, the same snipers. If at any stage you were spotted the odds against your getting back at all were extremely large

However, Harry was a scout, and it was his job. In the afternoon of that day I met him somewhere in the line and made some would-be jocular remark about his night's work. He seemed to me a little worried, preoccupied, and answered shortly. Hewett was sitting near, shaving in the sun, and said to him : ' You 're a nasty, cold-blooded fellow, Harry, crawling about like a young snake every night. But I suppose you like it.'

Harry said slowly, with a casual air : ' Well, so I did, but I must say that strafe the other night put the wind up me properly—and when

I went out last night I found I was thinking all
the time, " Suppose they did that again ? "
. . . and when I got on the top of a ridge or
anywhere a bit exposed, I kept imagining
what it would be like if all those machine-guns
started just then . . . simply dashed into a shell-
hole . . . and I found myself working for safe
spots where one would be all right in case of
accidents. . . . Sort of lost confidence, you
know.'

It was all said in a matter-of-fact manner,
as if he was saying, ' I don't like marmalade
so much as I used to do,' and there was no
suggestion that he was not ready to go and
look in the Boche front line or the Unter den
Linden, if necessary. But I was sorry about
this. I told him that he must not imagine ;
that that strafe was a unique affair, never
likely to be repeated. But when I went back
to the dug-out I spoke to the Colonel.

That night I went up with Harry to Foster
Alley, and watched him writhing away into
the grey gloom. There were many stars, and
you could follow him for thirty yards. And
as I watched I wondered, ' Is he thinking,
" *Supposing they do that again ?* " and when
he gets over near the wire, will he be thinking,
" *What would happen if they saw me now ?* "
If so,' I said, ' God help him,' and went back
to Headquarters.

Three hours later he came into the dug-out, where I sat with the Colonel making out an Intelligence Report. He was very white and tired, and while he spoke to the Colonel he stood at the bottom of the muddy steps with his head just out of the candlelight. All the front of his tunic was muddy, and there were two rents in his breeches.

He said, ' Very sorry, sir, but I couldn't get through. I got pretty close to the wire, but couldn't find a gap.' ' Was there much firing ? ' said the Colonel. ' The usual two snipers and a machine-gun on the left ; from what I heard I should say there were a good many men in that part of the trench—but I couldn't swear.' Now what the Colonel had wanted was some-body who *could* swear ; that was what the Brigade wanted ; so he was not pleased. But he was a kind, understanding fellow, and all he said was, ' Well, I 'm sorry, too, Penrose, but no doubt you did your best.' And he went to bed.

Then I opened some Perrier (we still had Perrier then), and gave Harry a strong whisky, and waited. For I knew that there was more. He talked for a little, as usual, about the mud, and the Boche line, and so on, and then he said : ' What I told the Colonel was perfectly true—I did get pretty close to the wire, and there wasn't a gap to be seen—but that wasn't

the whole of it . . . I couldn't face it. . . .
The truth is, that show the other night was too
much for me. . . . I found myself lying in a
shell-hole pretending to myself that I was
listening, and watching, and so on, but really
absolutely stuck, trying to *make* myself go on
. . . and I couldn't. . . . I'm finished as a
scout . . . that's all.'

Well, it was all for the present. No thinking, human C.O. is going to run a man in for
being beaten by a job like that. It is a
specialist's affair, like firing a gun. It is his
business to put the right man on the job, and
if he doesn't, he can't complain.

So we made Harry Lewis Gun officer. And
that was the first stage.

VIII

SOON after that we went down to the Somme. It was autumn then, and all that desolate area of stark brown earth was wet and heavy and stinking. Down the Ancre valley there were still some leaves in Thiepval Wood, and the tall trees along the river were green and beautiful in the thin October sun. But the centre of battle was coming up to that valley ; in a month the green was all gone, and there was nothing to see but the endless uniform landscape of tumbled earth and splintered trunks, and only the big shells raising vain waterspouts in the wide pools of the Ancre gave any brightness to the tired eye.

But you know about all this. Every Englishman has a picture of the Somme in his mind, and I will not try to enlarge it. We were glad, in a way, to go there, not in the expectation of liking it, but on the principle of Henry V's speech on the eve of St. Crispin. We saw ourselves in hospitals, or drawing-rooms, or bars, saying, ' Yes, we were six months on the Somme ' (as indeed we were) ; we were going to be ' in the swing.' But it was very vile. After Souchez it was real war again, and many Souchez reputations wilted there and died.

Yet with all its horror and discomfort and fear that winter was more bearable than the Gallipoli summer. For, at the worst, there was a little respite, spasms of repose. You came back sometimes to billets, cold, bare, broken houses, but still houses, where you might make a brave blaze of a wood fire and huddle round it in a cheery circle with warm drinks and a song or two. And sometimes there were estaminets and kind French women ; or you went far back to an old château, perched over the village, and there was bridge and a piano and guests at Headquarters. Civilization was within reach, and sometimes you had a glimpse of it—and made the most of it.

But we had a bad time, as every one did. After a stiff three weeks of holding a nasty bit of the line, much digging of assembly trenches, and carrying in the mud, we took our part in a great battle. I shall not tell you about it (it is in the histories) ; but it was a black day for the battalion. We lost 400 men and 20 officers, more than twice the total British casualties at Omdurman. Hewett was killed and six other officers, the Colonel and twelve more were wounded. Eustace showed superb courage with a hideous wound. Harry and myself survived. Now I had made a mistake about Harry. After that scouting episode at

Souchez I told myself that his ' nerve ' was
gone, that for a little anyhow he would be no
good in action. But soon after we got to the
Somme he had surprised me by doing a very
good piece of work under fire. We were
digging a new ' jumping-off ' line in No Man's
Land, two hundred men at work at once.
They were spotted, the Boches dropped some
Minnies about, and there was the beginning
of a slight stampede—you know the sort of
thing—mythical orders to ' Retire ' came along.
All Harry did was to get the men back and
keep them together, and keep them digging,
the officer's job—but he did very well, and to
me, as I say, surprisingly well. The truth was,
as I afterwards perceived, that only what I
may call his ' scouting ' nerve was gone. It is
a peculiar kind of super-nerve, as I have tried
to show, and losing it he had lost a very valuable
quality, but that was all at present.

Or I may put it another way. There is
a theory held among soldiers, which I will
call the theory of the favourite fear. Every
civilian has his favourite fear, death by burning
or by drowning, the fear of falling from a great
height, or being mangled in a machine—
something which it makes him shiver to think
about. Among soldiers such special fears are
even more acute, though less openly confessed,
but in the evenings men will sometimes lie on

the straw in the smoky barns and whisper the things of which they are most afraid.

It is largely a matter of locality and circumstance. In Gallipoli, where the Turks' rapid musketry fire was almost incredibly intense and their snipers uncannily accurate, men would say that they hated bullets, but shell-fire left them unmoved. The same men travelled to France and found rifle-fire practically extinct but gun-power increasingly terrible, and rapidly reversed their opinions.

More often, however, there has been some particular experience which, out of a multitude of shocks, has been able to make a lasting impression, and leave behind it the favourite fear.

One man remembers the death of a friend caught by the gas without his gas mask and is possessed with the fear that he may one day forget his own and perish in the same agony. And such is the effect on conduct of these obsessions that this man will neglect the most ordinary precautions against other dangers, will be reckless under heavy shell-fire, but will not move an inch without his respirator.

With others it is the fear of being left to die between the lines, caught on the wire and riddled by both sides, the fear of snipers, of 5·9's, even of whizz-bangs. One man feels safe in the open, but in the strongest dug-out has a horror that it may be blown in upon him.

There is the fear of the empty trench, where, like a child on the dark staircase, another man is convinced that there are enemies lying behind the parapet ready to leap upon him ; and there is the horror of being killed on the way down from the line after a relief.

But most to be pitied of all the men I have known, was one who had served at Gallipoli in the early days ; few men then could have an orderly burial in a recognized ground, but often the stretcher-bearers buried them hastily where they could in and about the lines. This man's fear was that one day a sniper would get him in the head ; that unskilled companions would pronounce his death sentence, and that he would wake up, perhaps within a few yards of his own trench, and know that he was buried but not dead.

That was how it was with Harry. The one thing he could not face at present was crawling lonely in the dark with the thought of that tornado of bullets in his head. Nothing else frightened him—now—more than it frightened the rest of us, though, God knows, that was enough.

So that he did quite well in this battle in a sound, undistinguished way. He commanded a platoon for the occasion, and took them through the worst part of the show without exceptional losses ; and he got as far as any

of the regiment got. He held out there for
two days under very heavy shell-fire, with a
mixed lot of men from several battalions, and
a couple of strange officers. In the evening
of the second day we were to be relieved, and
being now in command I sent him down with
a runner to Brigade Headquarters to fix up
a few points about our position and the relief.
There was a terrific barrage to pass, but both
of them got through. When his business was
done he started back to rejoin the battalion.
By that time it was about eleven o'clock at
night, and the relief was just beginning ; there
was no reason why he should have come back
at all ; indeed, the Brigade Major told him he
had better not, had better wait there in the
warm dug-out, and join us as we passed down.
Now when a man has been through a two-
days' battle of this kind, has had no sleep and
hardly any food for two days, and finished up
with a two-mile trudge over a stony wilderness
of shell-holes, through a vicious barrage of
heavy shells ; when after all this he finds himself, worn and exhausted so that he can hardly
stand, but safe and comfortable in a deep
dug-out where there are friendly lights and the
soothing voices of calm men ; and when he has
the choice of staying there, the right side of
the barrage, till it is time to go out to rest, or
of going back through that same barrage.

staggering into the same shell-holes, with the immediate prospect *of doing it all over again with men to look after as well as himself*—well, the temptation is almost irresistible. But Harry did resist it—I can't tell you how—and he started back. The barrage was worse than ever, all down the valley road, and, apparently, when they came near the most dangerous part, Harry's runner was hit by a big splinter and blown twenty yards. There were no stretchers unoccupied for five miles, and it was evident that the boy—he was only a kid—would die in a little time. He knew it himself, but he was very frightened in that hideous valley where the shells still fell, and he begged Harry not to leave him. And so we came upon them as we stumbled down, thanking our stars we were through the worst of it, Harry and the runner crouched together in a shell-hole, with the heart of the barrage blazing and roaring sixty yards off, and stray shells all round.

From a military or, indeed, a common-sense point of view, it was a futile performance—the needless risk of a valuable officer's life.

They do not give decorations for that kind of thing. But I was glad he had stayed with that young runner.

And I only tell you this to show you how wrong I was, and how much stuff he had in him still.

II

And now Colonel Philpott comes into the story. I wish to God he had kept out of it altogether. He was one of a class of officer with which our division was specially afflicted —at least we believed so, if only for the credit of the British Army ; for if they were typical of the Old Army I do not know how we came out of 1914 with as much honour as we did. But I am happy to know they were not. We called them the Old Duds, and we believed that for some forgotten sin of ours, or because of a certain strong ' Temporary ' spirit we had, they were dumped upon us by way of penalty. We had peculiarly few Regular officers, and so perhaps were inclined to be extra critical of these gentlemen. Anyhow, at one time they came in swarms, lazy, stupid, ignorant men, with many years of service—retired, reserve, or what not—but no discoverable distinction either in intellect, or character, or action. And when they had told us about Simla and all the injustices they had suffered in the matter of promotion or pay, they ousted some young and vigorous Temporary fellow who at least knew something of fighting, if there were stray passages in the King's Regulations which he did not know by heart ; and in about a week their commands were discontented and slack. In about two months they were evacuated sick (for they had no 'guts,' most of them), and that was the finest moment of their careers—for them and for us.

Lt.-Col. (Temp'y) W. K. Philpott (Substantive Captain) out-dudded them all, though, to give him his due, he had more staying power than most of them. He took over the battalion when Colonel Roberts was wounded, and the contrast was painfully acute. I was his adjutant for twelve months in all, and an adjutant knows most things about his C.O. He was a short, stoutish fellow, with beady eyes and an unsuccessful moustache, slightly grey, like a stubble-field at dawn. He had all the exaggerated respect for authority and his superiors of the old-school Regular, with none of its sincerity ; for while he said things about the Brigadier which no colonel should say before a junior officer, he positively cringed when they met. And though he bullied defaulters, and blustered about his independence before juniors, there was no superior military goose to whom he would have said the most diffident 'Bo!' He was lazy beyond words, physically and mentally, but to see him double out of the mess when a general visited the village was an education.

Then, of course, he believed very strongly in 'The Book,' not Holy Writ, but all that

mass of small red publications which expound
the whole art of being a soldier in a style cal-
culated to invest with mystery the most obvious
truths. ' It says it in The Book ' was his great
gambit—and a good one too. Yet he betrayed
the most astonishing ignorance of The Book.
Any second-lieutenant could have turned him
inside out in two minutes on Field Service
Regulations, and just where you expected him
to be really efficient and knowledgeable, the
conduct of trials, and Military Law, and so on,
he made the most elementary howlers.

But ignorance is easily forgivable if a man
will work, if a man will learn. But he would
neither. He left everything to somebody
else, the second-in-command, the adjutant,
the orderly-room. He would not say what
he wanted (he very seldom knew), and when
in despair you made out his orders for him
he invariably disagreed ; when he disagreed
he was as obstinate as a mule, without being
so clever. When he did agree it took half an
hour to explain the simplest arrangement.
If you asked him to sign some correspondence
for the Brigade, he was too lazy and told you
to sign it yourself ; and when you did that he
apologized to the Brigade for the irregularities
of his adjutant—' a Temporary fellow, you
know.' For he had an ill-concealed contempt
for all Temporaries ; and that was perhaps

one reason why we disliked him so much.
He would not believe that a young officer, who
had not spent twenty years drinking in mess-
rooms, could have any military value whatever. Moreover, it annoyed him intensely
(and here he had my sympathy) to see such
men enjoying the same pay or rank as he had
enjoyed during the protracted period of his
captaincy. And having himself learned practically nothing during that long lotus-time, it
was inconceivable to him that any man, however vigorous or intelligent, could have learned
anything in two years of war.

Now let me repeat that I do not believe him
to be typical of the Old Army, I know he was
not (thank God) ; but this is a history of what
happened to Harry, and Colonel Philpott was
one of the things which happened—very
forcibly. So I give him to you as we found
him, and since he may be alive I may say that
his name is fictitious, though there are,
unhappily, so many of him alive that I have
no fears that he will recognize himself. He
would not be the same man if he did.

We went out for a fortnight's rest after that
battle, and Harry had trouble with him almost
at once. He had amused and irritated Harry
from the first—the Old Duds always did—
for his respect for authority was very civilian
and youthful in character ; he took a man

for what he was, and if he decided he was good stood by him loyally for ever after ; if he did not he was severe, not to say intolerant.

Philpott's arrogance on the subject of Temporaries annoyed him intensely ; it also annoyed us all, and this I think it was that made him say a very unfortunate thing. He was up before the C.O. with some trifling request or other (I forget what), and somehow the question of his seniority and service came up.   Incidentally, Harry remarked, quite mildly, that he believed he was nearly due for promotion. Colonel Philpott gave as close an imitation of a lively man as I ever saw him achieve ; he nearly had ·a fit.   I forget all he said—he thundered for a long time, banging his fist on the King's Regulations, and knocking everything off the rickety table—but this was the climax :

' Promotion, by God ! and how old are you, young man ? and how much service have you seen ?   Let me tell you this, Master Penrose, when I was your age I hadn't begun to *think* about promotion, and I did fifteen years as a captain—fifteen solid years ! '

' You amaze me, sir,' said Harry.

It was very wrong ; and unfortunate.

III

When we went back to the line, Harry was detailed for many working-parties ; and some of them, particularly the first, were very nasty. The days of comfortable walking in communication trenches were over. We were in captured ground churned up by our own fire, and all communication with the front was over the open, over the shell-holes. Harry was told off to take a ration-party, carrying rations up to the battalion in the line, a hundred men. These were bad jobs to do. It meant three-quarters of a mile along an uphill road, heavily shelled ; then there was a mile over the shell-hole country, where there were no landmarks or duckboards, nor anything to guide you. For a single man in daylight, with a map, navigation was difficult enough in this uniform wilderness until you had been over it a time or two ; to go over it for the first time, in the dark, with a hundred men carrying heavy loads, was the kind of thing that makes men transfer to the Flying Corps. Harry got past the road with the loss of three men only ; there, at any rate, you went straight ahead, however slowly. But when he left the road his real troubles began. It was pitch dark and drizzling, and the way was still uphill. With those unhappy carrying-parties, where three-fourths of the men carried two heavy sacks of bread and tinned meat and other food, and the rest two petrol tins of water, or a jar of rum, or rifle oil, or whale oil, besides a rifle, and a bandolier, and two respirators, and a great-coat—you must move with exquisite slowness, or you will lose your whole party in a hundred yards. And even when you are just putting one foot in front of another, moving so slowly that it maddens you, there are halts and hitches every few yards : a man misses his footing and slides down into a crater with his awful load ; the hole is full of foul green water, and he must be hauled out quickly lest he drown. Half-way down the line a man halts to ease his load, or shift his rifle, or scratch his nose ; when he goes on he can see no one ahead of him, and the cry ' Not in touch ' comes sullenly up to the front. Or you cross the path of another party, burdened as yours. In the dark, or against the flaring skyline, they look like yours, bent, murky shapes with bumps upon them, and some of your men trail off with the other party. And though you pity your men more than yourself, it is difficult sometimes to be gentle with them, difficult not to yield to the intense exasperation of it all, and curse foolishly.

But Harry was good with his men, and they stumbled on, slipping, muttering, with a dull ache at the shoulders and a dogged rage in their hearts. He was trying to steer by the compass, and he was aiming for a point given him on the map, the rendezvous for the party he was to meet. This point was the junction of three trenches, but as all trenches thereabouts had been so blotted out as to be almost indistinguishable from casual shell-holes, it was not so good a rendezvous as it had seemed to the Brigade However, Harry managed to find it, or believed that he had found it—for in that murk and blackness nothing was certain ; if he had found it, the other party had not, for there was no one there. They might be late, they might be lost, they might be waiting elsewhere. So Harry sent out a scout or two and waited, while the men lay down in the muddy ruins of the trench and dozed unhappily. And while they waited. the Boche, who had been flinging big shells about at random since dusk, took it into his head to plaster these old trenches with 5·9's. Harry ran, or floundered, along the line, telling the men to lie close where they were. There was indeed nothlng else to do, but it gave the men confidence, and none of them melted away. As he ran, a big one burst very near and knocked him flat, but he was untouched ; it is marvellous how local the effect of H.E. can be. For about ten minutes they had a bad time, and then it ceased, suddenly.

And now was one of those crucial moments which distinguish a good officer from a bad, or even an ordinary officer. It was easy to say, ' Here I am at the rendezvous ' (by this time Harry had got his bearings a little by the lights, and knew he was in the right spot) ' with these bloody rations ; the men are done and a bit shaken ; so am I ; the other people haven't turned up ; if they want their rations they can damned well come here and get them ; I 've done my part, and I 'm going home.' But a real good officer, with a con-science and an imagination, would say : ' Yes —but I 've been sent up here to get these rations to the men in the line ; my men will have a rest to-morrow, and some sleep, and some good food ; the men in the line now will still be in the line, with no sleep, and little rest, and if these rations are left here in the mud and not found before dawn, they 'll have no food either ; and whatever other people may do or not do, it 's up to me to get these rations up there somehow, if we have to walk all night and carry them right up to the front line ourselves, and I 'm not going home till I 've done it.' I don't know, but I think that that 's the sort of thing Harry said to himself ; and anyhow after the row with Philpott he was particularly anxious to make good. So he got his men out and told them about it all,

and they floundered on. It was raining hard
now, with a bitter wind when they passed the
crest of the hill. Harry had a vague idea of
the direction of the line so long as they were
on the slope; but on the flat, when they
had dodged round a few hundred shell-holes,
halting and going on and halting again, all
sense of direction departed, and very soon
they were hopelessly lost. The flares were no
good, for the line curved, and there seemed to
be lights all around, going up mistily through
the rain in a wide circle. Once you were
properly lost the compass was useless, for
you might be in the Boche lines, you might be
anywhere. . . . At such moments a kind of
mad, desperate self-pity, born of misery and
weariness and rage, takes hold of the infantryman, and if he carries a load he is truly ready
to fall down and sleep where he is—or die.
And in the wretched youth in charge there
is a sense of impotence and responsibility that
makes his stomach sink within him. Some
of the men began to growl a little, but Harry
held on despairingly. And then by God's
grace they ran into another party, an N.C.O.
and a few men; these were the party—or
some of them—that should have met them at
the rendezvous; they too had been lost
and were now wandering back to the line.
Well, Harry handed over the rations and

turned home, well pleased with himself. He was too sick of the whole affair, and it was too dark and beastly to think of getting a receipt. It was a pity; for while he trudged home, the N.C.O., as we afterwards heard, was making a mess of the whole business. Whether he had not enough men or perhaps lost them, or miscalculated the amount of rations or what is not clear, but half of all that precious food was found lying in the mud at noon the next day when it was too late, and half the battalion in the line went very short. Then the Colonel rang up Philpott, and complained bitterly about the conduct of the officer in charge of our ration-party. Philpott sent for Harry and accused him hotly of dumping the rations carelessly anywhere, of not finishing his job.

Harry gave his account of the affair quite simply, without enlarging on the bad time he had had, though that was clear enough to a man with any knowledge. *But he could not show a receipt.* Philpott was the kind of man who valued receipts more than righteousness. He refused to believe Harry's straightforward tale, cursed him for a lazy swine, and sent him to apologize to the Colonel of the Blanks. That officer did listen to Harry's story, believed it, and apologized to *him.* Harry was a little soothed, but from that day I know there was a great bitterness in his heart. For he had done a difficult job very well, and had come back justly proud of himself and his men. And to have the work wasted by a bungling N.C.O., and his word doubted by a Philpott. . . .

And that I may call the beginning of the second stage.

IX

FOR after that Harry began to be in a bad way again. That shelling in the night and the near concussion of the shell that knocked him over had been one of those capital shocks of which I have spoken. From that time on, shell-fire in the open became a special terror, a new favourite fear; afterwards he told me so. And all that winter we had shell-fire in the open—even the 'lines' were not trenches, only a string of scattered shell-holes garrisoned by a few men. Everywhere, night and day, you had that naked feeling.

Yet in France, at the worst, given proper rest and variety, with a chance to nurse his courage and soothe his nerves, a resolute man could struggle on a long time after he began to crack. But Harry had no rest, no chance. The *affaire Philpott* was having a rich harvest. For about three weeks in the February of that awful winter the battalion was employed solely on working-parties, all sorts of them, digging, carrying, behind the line, in the line, soft jobs, terrible jobs. Now as adjutant I used to take particular care that the safe jobs in the rear should be fairly shared among the companies in a rough rotation, and that no

officers or men should have too many of the
bad ones—the night carrying-parties to the
front line. But about now Colonel Philpott
began to exert himself about these parties ;
he actually issued orders about the arrangements, and whether by accident or design,
his orders had this particular effect that
Harry took about three times as many of the
dangerous parties as anybody else. We were
in a country of rolling down with long trough-
like valleys or ravines between. To get to the
front line you had to cross two of these valleys,
and in each of them the Boche put a terrific
barrage all night, and every night. The
second one—the Valley of Death—was about
as near to Inferno as I wish to see, for it was
enfiladed from both ends, and you had shell-
fire from three directions. Well, for three
weeks Harry took a party through this valley
four or five nights a week. . . . Each party
meant a double passage through two corners
of hell, with a string of weary men to keep
together and encourage and command, with
all that maddening accumulation of difficulties I have tried already to describe . . . and
at the end of that winter, after all he had done,
it was too much. I protested to the Colonel,
but it was no good. ' Master Penrose can go
on with these parties,' he said, ' till he learns
how to do them properly.'

After ten days of this Harry began to be afraid of himself ; or, as he put it, ' I don't know if I can stand much more of this.' All his old distrust of himself, which lately I think he had very successfully kept away, came creeping back. But he made no complaint ; he did not ask me to intercede with Philpott. The more he hated and feared these parties, the worse he felt, the keener became his determination to stick it out, to beat Philpott at his own game. Or so I imagine. For by the third week there was no doubt ; what is called his ' nerve ' was clean gone ; or, as he put it to me in the soldier's tongue, ' I 've got complete wind-up.' He would have given anything—except his pride—to have escaped one of those parties ; he thought about them all day. I did manage, in sheer defiance of Philpott, to take him off one of them ; but it was only sheer dogged will-power, and perhaps the knowledge that we were to be relieved the following week, which carried him through to the end of it.

If we had not gone out I don't know what would have happened. But I can guess.

II

And so Philpott finally broke his nerve. But he was still keen and resolute to go on, in

spite of the bitterness in his heart.   Philpott
—and other things—had still to break his
spirit.   And the 'other things' were many
that winter.   It was a long, cold, comfortless
winter.   Billets became more and more broken
and windowless and lousy ; firewood vanished,
and there was little coal.   On the high slopes
there was a bitter wind, and men went sick in
hundreds—pneumonia, fever, frost-bite.   All
dug-outs were damp and chilling and greasy
with mud, or full of the acrid smoke of damp
wood that tortured the eyes.   There were
night advances in the snow, where lightly
wounded men perished of exposure before
dawn.   For a fortnight we lived in tents on a
hill-top covered with snow.

And one day Harry discovered he was lousy.

Then, socially, though it seems a strange
thing to say, these were dull days for Harry.
Few people realize how much an infantryman's life is lightened if he has companions
of his own kind—not necessarily of the same
class, though it usually comes to that—but
of the same tastes and education and experience
—men who make the same kind of jokes.   In
the line it matters little, a man is a man, as
the Press will tell you.   But in the evenings,
out at rest, it was good and cheering to sit
with the Old Crowd and exchange old stories
of Gallipoli and Oxford and London ; even

to argue with Eustace about the Public Schools ; to be with men who liked the same songs, the same tunes on the gramophone, who did not always ask for ' My Dixie Bird ' or ' The Green Woman ' waltz. . . . And now there was none of the Old Crowd left, only Harry and myself, Harry with a company now, and myself very busy at Headquarters. And Harry's company were very dull men, promoted N.C.O.'s mostly, good fellows all—very good in the line—but they were not the Old Crowd. Now, instead of those great evenings we used to have, with the white wine, and the music, and old George dancing, evenings that have come down in the history of the battalion as our battles have done, evenings that kept the spirit strong in the blackest times—there were morose men with wooden faces sitting silently over some whisky and Battalion Orders.

And Hewett was dead, the laughing, lovable Hewett. That was the black heart of it. When a man becomes part of the great machine, he is generally supposed—I know not why— to surrender with his body his soul and his affections and all his human tendernesses. But it is not so.

We never talked of Hewett very much. Only there was for ever a great gap. And sometimes, when we tried to be cheerful in the

11

evenings, as in the old times, and were not, we said to each other—Harry and I—' I wish to God that he was here.' Yet for long periods I forgot Hewett. Harry never forgot him.

Then there was something about which I may be wrong, for Harry never mentioned it, and I am only guessing from my own opinion. In two years of war he had won no kind of medal or distinction—except a ' mention ' in despatches, which is about as satisfying as a caraway-seed to a starving man. In Gallipoli he had done things which in France in modern times would have earned an easy decoration. But they were scarce in those days ; and in France he had done much dogged and difficult work, and a few very courageous, but in a military sense perfectly useless things, nothing dramatic, nothing to catch the eye of the Brigade. I don't know whether he minded much, but I felt it myself very keenly ; for I knew that he had started with ambitions ; and here were fellows with not half his service, or courage, or capacity, just ordinary men with luck, ablaze with ribbon. . . . Any one who says he cares nothing about medals is a hypocrite, though most of us care very little. But if you believe you have done well, and not only is there nothing to show for it, but nothing to show that other people believe it, you can't help caring.

And then, on top of it, when you have a genuine sense of bitter injustice, when you know that your own most modest estimate of yourself is exalted compared with the estimate of the man who commands you—you begin to have black moods.

III

Harry had black moods. All these torments accumulated and broke his spirit. He lost his keenness, his cheerfulness, and his health. Once a man starts on that path, his past history finds him out, like an old wound. Some men take to drink and are disgraced. In Harry's case it was Gallipoli. No man who had a bad time in that place ever ' got over ' it in body or soul. And when France or some other campaign began to work upon them, it was seen that there was something missing in their resisting power ; they broke out with old diseases and old fears . . . the legacies of Gallipoli.

Harry grew pale, and nervous, and hunted to look at ; and he had a touch of dysentery. But the worst of the poison was in his mind and heart. For a long time, as I have said, since he felt the beginning of those old doubts, and saw himself starting downhill, he had striven anxiously to keep his name high in

men's opinion ; for all liked him and believed
in him. He had been ready for anything, and
done his work with a conscientious pride.
But now this bitterness was on him, he seemed
to have ceased to care what happened or what
men thought of him. He had unreasonable
fits of temper ; he became distrustful and
cynical. I thought then, sometimes, of the
day when he had looked at Troy and wanted
to be like Achilles. It was painful to me to
hear him talking as Eustace used to talk, suspicious, intolerant, incredulous. . . . I thought
how Harry had once hated that kind of talk,
and it was most significant of the change that
had come over the good companion I had
known. Yet sometimes, when the sun shone,
and once when we rode back into Albert and
dined quietly alone, that mask of bitterness
fell away ; there were flashes of the old cheerful Harry, and I had hopes. I hoped Philpott
would be killed.

IV

But he survived, for he was very careful.
And though, as I have said, he stuck it for a
long time, he was by no means the gallant fire-
eater you would have imagined from his treatment of defaulters. Once round the line just
before dawn was enough for him in that sort of

country. ' Things are quiet then, and you can
see what 's going on.' He liked it best when
' things were quiet.' So did all of us, and I
don't blame him for that.

But that winter there was a thick crop of
S.I.W.'s. S.I.W. is the short title for a man who
has been ' evacuated' with self-inflicted wounds
—shot himself in the foot, or held a finger over
the muzzle of his rifle, or dropped a great boulder
on his foot—done himself any reckless injury to
escape from the misery of it all. It was always a
marvel to me that any man who could find
courage to do such things could not find courage
to go on ; I suppose they felt it would bring
them the certainty of a little respite, and beyond
that they did not care, for it was the uncertainty
of their life that had broken them. You could
not help being sorry for these men, even
though you despised them. It made you sick
to think that any man who had come volun-
tarily to fight for his country could be
brought so low, that humanity could be so
degraded exactly where it was being so
ennobled.

But Philpott had no such qualms. He was
ruthless, and necessarily so ; but, beyond that,
he was brutal, he bullied. When they came
before him, healed of their wounds, haggard,
miserable wisps of men, he kept them standing
there while he told them at length exactly how

low they had sunk (they knew that well enough, poor devils), and flung at them a rich vocabulary of abuse—words of cowardice and dishonour, which were strictly accurate but highly unnecessary. For these men were going back to duty now ; they had done their punishment—though the worst of it was still to come ; all they needed was a few quiet words of encouragement from a strong man to a weaker, a little human sympathy, and that appeal to a man's honour which so seldom fails if it is rightly made.

Well, this did not surprise me in Philpott ; he had no surprises for me by now. What did surprise me was Harry's intolerant, even cruel, comments on the cases of the S.I.W.'s. He had always had a real sympathy with the men, he knew the strange workings of their minds, and all the wretchedness of their lives ; he understood them. And yet here he was, as scornful, as Prussian, on the subject of S.I.W.'s as even Philpott. It was long before I understood this —I don't know that I ever did. But I thought it was this : that in these wrecks of men he recognized something of his own sufferings ; and recognizing the disease he was the more appalled by the remedy they took. The kind of thing that had led them to it was the kind of thing he had been through, was going through. There the connection ceased. There was no

such way out for him. But though it ceased,
the connection was so close that it was degrad-
ing. And this scorn and anger was a kind of
instinctive self-defence—put on to assure himself, to assure the world, that there was no
connection—none at all. . . . But I don't
know.

v

At the end of February I was wounded and
went home. Without any conceit, without
exaggerating our friendship, I may say that
this was the final blow for Harry. I was the
last of the Old Crowd ; I was the one man who
knew the truth of things as between him and
Philpott. And I went.

I was hit by a big shell at Whizz-Bang Corner,
and Harry saw me on the stretcher as we came
past D Company on the Bapaume Road. He
walked with me as far as the cookers, and was
full of concern for my wound, which was pretty
painful just then. But he bucked me up and
talked gaily of the good things I was going to.
And he said nothing of himself. But when he
left me there was a look about him—what is
the word ?—*wistful*—it is the only one—like a
dog left behind.

While I was still in hospital I had two letters
from the battalion. The first was from Harry,

a long wail about Philpott and the dullness of everybody now that the Old Crowd were extinct, though he seemed to have made good friends of some of the dull ones. At the end of that endless winter, when it seemed as if the spring would never come, they had pulled out of the line and ' trekked ' up north, so that there had been little fighting. They were now in shell-holes across the high ridge in front of Arras, preparing for an advance.

The other letter was from old Knight, the Quartermaster, dated two months after I left.

I will give you an extract :

' *Probably by now you will have seen or heard from young Penrose. He was hit on the 16th, a nasty wound in the chest from a splinter. . . . It was rather funny—not funny, but you know what I mean—how he got it. I was there myself though I didn't see it. I had been up to H.Q. to see about the rations, and there were a lot of us, Johnson (he is now Adj. in your place) and Fellowes, and so on, standing outside H.Q. (which is on a hill—what you people call a forward slope, I believe), and watching our guns bombarding the village. It was a remarkable sight, etc. etc.* [a long digression]. . . . *Then the Boche started shelling our hill ; he dropped them in pairs, first of all at the other end of the hill, about 500 yards off, and then nearer and nearer, about 20 yards at a time . . . . the line they were on was pretty*

*near to us, so we thought the dug-out would be a
good place to go to. . . . Penrose was just starting
to go back to his company when this began, and as
we went down somebody told him he 'd better wait a
bit.   But he said " No, he wanted to get back."   I
was the last down, and as I disappeared (pretty
hurriedly) I told him not to be a fool.   But all he
said was, " This is nothing, old bird—you wait till
you live up here ; I 'm going on."   The next
thing we heard was the hell of an explosion on top.
We ran up afterwards, and there he was, about
thirty yards off. . . . The funny thing is that I
understood he rather had the wind-up just now,
and was anything but reckless . . . in fact, some
one said he had the Dug-out Disease. . . . Otherwise, you 'd have said he wanted to be killed.   I
don't know why he wasn't, asking for it like that.
. . . Well, thank God I 'm a Q.M., etc. etc.'*

I read it all very carefully, and wondered.
' *You 'd have said he wanted to be killed.*'   I
wondered about that very much.

And there was a postscript which interested
me :

' *By the way, I hear Burnett's got the M.C.—
for Salvage, I believe !* '

X

I WAS six months in that hospital, and I did not see Harry for seven. For I was at Blackpool, and he at Lady Radmore's in Kensington. His was a quicker business than mine ; and when I had finished with the hospitals and the homes and came to London for a three weeks' laze, he was back at the Depot. Then he got seven days' leave for some mysterious reason (I think there was a draft leaving shortly, and everybody had some leave), and I dined twice with him at home. They had a little house in Chelsea, very tastefully furnished by Mrs. Penrose, whom I now saw for the first time. But I saw more of her that evening than I did of Harry, who was hopelessly entangled with two or three ' in-laws.' She was a dark, gentle little person, with brown, and rather sorrowful, eyes. When I first saw her I thought, ' She was never meant to be a soldier's wife,' but after we had talked a little, I added, ' But she is a good one.' She was clearly very much in love with Harry, and delighted to meet some one who had been with him in France, and was fond of him—for, like all wives, she soon discovered that. But all the time I felt that there were questions she

wanted to ask me, and could not. I will not
pretend to tell you how she was dressed, because
I don't know ; I seldom notice, and then I never
remember.   But she appealed to me very much,
and· I made up my mind to look after *her*
interests if I ever had the chance, if there was
ever a question between Harry and a single man.
I had no chance of a talk with Harry, and
noticed only that he seemed pretty fit again but
sleepless-looking.

The second night I went there was the last
night of Harry's leave.   If I had known that
when I was asked I think I should not have
gone ; for while it showed I was a privileged
person, it is a painful privilege to break in on
the ' last evening ' of husband and wife ; I know
those last evenings.   And though Harry was
only going back to the Depot in the morning, it
was known there had been heavy losses in the
regiment ; there was talk of a draft ; it might
well be the last evening of all.

I got there early, at Harry's request, about
half-past five, on a miserable gusty evening in
early November.   Harry was sitting in a kind
of study, library, or den, writing ; he looked less
well, and very sleepless about the eyes.

It was the anniversary of one of the great
battles of the regiment ; and we talked a little
of that day, as soldiers will, with a sort of
gloomy satisfaction.   Then Harry said, slowly :

' I 've been offered a job at the War Office—
by Major Mackenzie—Intelligence.'

' Oh,' I said, ' that 's very good.' (But I was
thinking more of Mrs. Harry than Harry.)

Harry went on, as if he had not heard. ' I
was writing to him when you came in. And I
don't know what to say.'

' Why not ? '

' Well,' he said, ' *you* know as well as any one
what sort of time I 've had, and how I 've been
treated—by Philpott and others. And I 've
had about enough of it. I remember telling
you once on the Peninsula that I thought myself
fairly brave when I first went out . . . and, my
God, so I was compared with what I am now.
. . . I suppose every one has his breaking-point,
and I've certainly had mine. . . . I simply feel
I can't face it again.'

' Very well,' I said, ' take the job and have
done with it. You 've done as much as you
can, and you can't do more. What 's the
trouble ? '

But he went on, seemingly to convince himself rather than me. ' I 've never got over
those awful working-parties in that —— valley ;
I had two or three 5·9's burst right on top of
me, you know . . . the Lord knows how I
escaped . . . and now I simply dream of them.
I dream of them every night . . . usually it 's
an enormous endless plain, full of shell-holes, of

course, and raining like hell, and I walk for miles (usually with you) looking over my shoulder, waiting for the shells to come . . . and then I hear that savage kind of high-velocity shriek, and I run like hell . . . only I can't run, of course, that 's the worst part . . . and I get into a ditch and lie there . . . and then one comes that I know by the sound is going to burst on top of me . . . and I wake up simply sweating with funk. I 've never told anybody but you about this, not even Peggy, but she says I wake her up sometimes, making an awful noise.'

He was silent for a little, and I had nothing to say.

' And then it 's all so different now, so damnably . . . dull. . . . I wouldn't mind if we could all go out together again . . . just the Old Crowd . . . so that we could have good evenings, and not care what happened. But now there 's nobody left (I don't expect they 'll let *you* go out again), only poor old Egerton—he 's back again . . . and I can't stand all those boot-faced N.C.O. officers and people like Philpott, and all the Old Duds. . . . You can't get away from it—the boot-faces *aren't* officers, and nothing will make them so . . . even the men can't stand them. And they get on my nerves. . . .

' It all gets on my nerves, the mud, and the

cold, and the futile Brigadiers, and all the damned eyewash we have nowadays . . . never having a decent wash, and being cramped up in a dug-out the size of a chest-of-drawers with four boot-faces . . . where you can't move without upsetting the candle and the food, or banging your head . . . and getting lousy. And all those endless ridiculous details you have to look after day after day . . . working-parties . . . haversack rations . . . has every man got his box-respirator ? . . . why haven't you cleaned your rifle ? . . . as if I cared a damn ! . . . No, I won't say that . . . but there you are, you see, it 's on my nerves. . . . But sometimes ' (and though I sympathized I was glad there was a ' but ') ' when I think of some of the bogus people who 've been out, perhaps once, and come home after three months with a nice blighty in the shoulder, and got a job, and stayed in it ever since . . . I feel I can't do that either, and run the risk of being taken for one of them. . . .'

' I don't think there 's any danger of that,' I remarked.

' I don't know—one " officeer " is the same as another to most people. . . . And then, you know, although you hate it, it does get hold of you somehow—out there . . . and after a bit, when you 've got used to being at home you get restless. . . . I know I did last time, and sometimes I do now. . . . I don't say I hunger for the battle, I never want to be in a " stunt " again . . . but you feel kind of " out of it " when you read the papers, or meet somebody on leave . . . you think of the amusing evenings we used to have. . . . And I rather enjoyed " trekking " about in the back areas . . . especially when I had a horse . . . wandering along on a good frosty day, and never sure what village you were going to sleep in . . . marching through Doullens with the band . . . estaminets, and talking French, and all the rest of it. . . .

' And then I think of a 5·9—and I know I 'm done for. . . . I 've got too much imagination, that 's the trouble (I hope you 're not fed up with all this, but I want your advice). . . . It 's funny, one never used to think about getting killed, even in the war . . . it seemed impossible somehow that *you yourself* could be killed (did you ever have that feeling ?) . . . though one was ready enough in those days . . . but now—even in the train the other day, going down to Bristol by the express, I found I was imagining what would happen if there was a smash . . things one reads of, you know . . . carriages catching fire, and so on . . . just " wind-up." And the question is—is it any *good* going out, if you 've got into that state ? . . . And if one says " No," is one just making

it an excuse? . . . It's no good telling a
military doctor all this . . . they'd just say,
" Haw, skrim-shanker ! what you want is some
fresh air and exercise, my son ! " . . . And for
all I know they may be right. . . . As a matter
of fact, I don't think I'm physically fit, really
. . . my own doctor says not . . . but you're
never examined properly before you go out, as
you know. . . . You all troop in by the dozen
at the last moment . . . and the fellow says,
" Feeling quite fit ? " . . . And if you've just
had a good breakfast and feel buckish, you say,
" Yes, thank you," and there you are. . . .
Unless you *ask* them to examine you you might
have galloping consumption for all they know,
and I'm damned if I'd ask them. . . . After
all, I suppose the system's right. . . . If a man
can stick it for a month or two in the line, he's
worth sending there if he's an officer . . . and
it doesn't matter to the country if he dies of
consumption afterwards. . . . But my trouble
is—*can* I stick it for a month or two . . . or
shall I go and do some awful thing, and let a lot
of fellows down ? . . . Putting aside my own
inclinations, which are probably pretty selfish,
what is it my duty to do ? . . . After friend
Philpott I don't know that I'm so keen on duty
as I was . . . but I do want to stick this ——
war out on the right line, if I can. . . . What
do *you* think ? '

' Before I answer that,' I said, ' there 's one consideration you seem to have overlooked— and that is Mrs. Penrose. . . . After all, you 're a married man, and that makes a difference, doesn't it ? '

' Well, does it ? I don't really see why it *should* make any difference about going out, or not going out . . . otherwise every shirker could run off and marry a wife, and live happily ever after. . . . But it certainly makes it a damned sight harder to decide . . . and it makes the hell of a difference when you 're out there. . . . You can make up your mind not to think of it when you 're at home . . . like this . . . but out there, when you 're cold and fed up, and just starting up the line with a working-party . . . you can't help thinking of it, and it makes things about ten times more difficult . . . and as you know, it 's jolly hard not to let it make a difference to what you do. . . . But, damn it, why did you remind me of that ? I didn't want to think about it.'

And then Mrs. Penrose came in, and we went down to dinner.

II

I did not enjoy that dinner. To begin with, I felt like a vulgar intruder on something that was almost sacred, and certainly very precious.

For all the signs of the ' last evening ' were there. The dishes we had were Harry's favourites, procured at I know not what trouble and expense by Mrs. Harry ; and she watched tremulously to see that he liked them. She had gone out and bought him a bottle of well-loved Moselle, for a special surprise, and some port ; which was a huge extravagance. But that was nothing, if these things could only give a special something to this meal which would make him remember it ; for the flowers he never saw, and the new dress went unnoticed for a long time. But I felt that it would all have gone much better, perhaps, if I had not been there, and I hoped she did not hate me.

And Harry was not at his best. The question he asked me I had had no time to answer, and he had not answered it himself. Through most of that dinner, which by all the rules should have been, superficially at least, cheerful and careless, as if there were no such thing as separation ahead, Harry was thoughtful and preoccupied. And I knew that he was still arguing with himself, ' What shall I say to Mackenzie ? Yes or No ? '—wandering up and down among the old doubts and resolutions and fears. . . . Mrs. Harry saw this as well as I . . . and, no doubt, she cursed me for being there, because in my presence she could not ask him what worried him.

But the Moselle began to do its work : Harry talked a little and noticed the new dress, and we all laughed a lot at the pudding, which came up in such a curious shape. We were very glad to laugh at something.

Then Mrs. Harry spoke of some people in tne regiment of whom she had heard a good deal—George Dawson, and Egerton, and old Colonel Roberts. I knew that in a minute we should stumble into talking about the trenches or shells, or some such folly, and have Harry gloomy and brooding again. I could not stand that, and I did not think Mrs. Harry could, so I plunged recklessly into the smoother waters of life in France. I told them the old story about General Jackson and the billet-guard ; and then we came on to the famous night at Forceville, and other historic battalion orgies—the dinner at Monchy Breton, when we put a row of candles on the floor of the tent for footlights, and George and a few subalterns made a perfect beauty chorus. Those are the things one likes to remember about active service, and I was very glad to remember them then. The special port came in and was a great success ; Harry warmed up, and laughed over those old gaieties, and was in great form. At that moment I think his answer to Major Mackenzie would have been definitely ' No.'

Mrs. Harry laughed very much too, and said

she envied us the amusing times we had together
' out there.'   ' You men have all the fun.'
And that made me feel a heartless ass for having
started on that topic.   For I knew that when
Harry was away there was little ' fun ' for her ;
and whether he was lying on his stomach in a
shell-hole, or singing songs in an estaminet, not
thinking much of his wife, perhaps, except when
they drank ' Sweethearts and Wives '—it was
all one uniform, hideous wait for her.   So I
think it was hollow laughter for Mrs. P. . . .

Moreover, though I did not know how much
she knew about Harry's difficulties, the ' job '
and so on, I felt sure that with the extraordinary
instinct of a wife she scented something of the
conflict that was going on ; and she knew
vaguely that this exaggerated laudation of the
amenities of France meant somehow danger to
her. . . . So that just as I was beginning to
congratulate myself on the bucking up of Harry,
I tardily perceived that between us we were
wounding the wife.   And I more than ever
wished myself anywhere than sitting at that
pretty table with the shaded lights.

Well, we nearly finished the port—Harry still
in excellent form—and went upstairs.   Harry
went off to look for smokes or something, and I
knew at once that Mrs. Harry was going to ask
me questions about him.   You know how a
woman stands in front of the fire, and looks

down, and kind of paws the fender with one foot when she is going to say something confidential. Then she looks up suddenly, and you re done. Mrs. Harry did that, and I was done. At any other time I should have loved to talk to her about Harry, but that night I felt it was dangerous ground.

' How do you think Harry is looking ? ' she said. ' You probably know better than I do, nowadays.'

I said I thought he seemed pretty fit, considering all things.

' Do you think he 'll have to go out again ? ' she asked. ' I don't think he ought to—but they seem so short of men still. He 's not really strong, you know.'

So she knew nothing about the ' job '; and this put me in a hole. For if I told her about it, and he did not take it, but went out again, the knowledge would be a standing torture to her. On the other hand, I *wanted* him to take it, I thought he ought to—and if she knew about it she might be able to make him. Wives can do a great deal in that way. But that would be disloyal to Harry.

Well, I temporized with vague answers while I wrestled with this problem, and she told me more about Harry. ' You know, he has the most *terrible* dreams . . . wakes up screaming at night, and quite frightens me. And I don't think they ought to be *allowed* to go out again when they 're like that. . . . I don't *want* him to go out again. . . . At least,' she added half-heartedly (as a kind of concession to convention), ' if it 's his duty, of course . . .' Then, defiantly, ' No, I *don't* want him to go . . . anyhow . . . I think he 's done his bit . . . hasn't he, Mr. Benson ? '

' He has, indeed,' I said, with sincerity at last.

' Well, you have some influence with him. Can't you——'

But then Harry came in, and I had lost my chance. I have noticed that while on the stage conversations which must necessarily be private are invariably concluded without interruption ; in private life, and especially private houses, they are always interrupted long before the end.

Mrs. Harry went to the piano, and Harry and I sat down to smoke ; and since it was the last night Harry was allowed to smoke his pipe. The way Mrs. Harry said that nearly made me weep.

So I sat there and watched Harry, and his wife played and played—soft, melancholy, homesick things (Chopin, I think), that leagued with the wine and the warm fire and the deep chairs in an exquisite conspiracy of repose. She played for a long time, but I saw that she too was watching. And the fancy came to me that she was fighting for Harry, fighting, perhaps unconsciously, that vague danger she had seen at dinner, when it had beaten her . . . fighting it with this music that made war seem so distant and home so lovable.

And soon I began to see that she was winning. For when she began playing Harry had sat down, a little restless again, and fidgeted, as if the music reminded him of good things too much . . . and his eyes wandered round the room and took in all the familiar things, like a man saying good-bye—the old chair with the new chintz, and the yellow curtains, and the bookcase his father left him—and the little bookcase where his history books were (he looked a long time at them) . . . and the fire-light shining on the piano . . . and his wife playing and playing. . . . And when he had looked at her, quickly, he sat up and poked the fire fiercely, and sat back, frowning. He was wondering again. This music was being too much for him. Then she stopped, and looked across at Harry—and smiled.

When she played again it was, I think, a nocturne of Chopin's (God knows which—but it was very peaceful and homesick), and as I watched, I made sure that she had won. For there came over Harry a wonderful repose. He no longer frowned or fidgeted, or raised his eyebrows in the nervous way he had, but lay back in a kind of abandonment of content. And I said to myself, ' He has decided—he will say " Yes " to Mackenzie.'

Mrs. Harry, perhaps, also perceived it. For after a little she stopped and came over to us. And then I did a fateful thing. There was a copy of *The Times* lying by my chair, and, because of the silence that was on us, I picked it up and looked aimlessly at it.

The first thing I saw was the Casualty List, buried in small type among some vast advertisements of patent foods. I glanced down the list in that casual manner which came to us when we knew that all our best friends were already dead or disposed of. Then my eye caught the name of the regiment and the name of a man I knew. CAPTAIN EGERTON, V.R. Killed. There was another near it, and another, and many more ; the list was thick with them. And the other battalions in the Brigade had many names there—fellows one had relieved in the line, or seen in billets, or talked with in the Cocktail Café at Nœux-les-Mines. There must have been a massacre in the Brigade . . . ten officers killed and ten wounded in our lot alone.

I suppose I made that vague murmur of rage and regret which slips out of you when you read these things, for Harry looked up and asked, ' What 's that ? ' I gave him the paper, and he too looked down that list. . . . Only two of those names were names of the Old Crowd, and many of them were the dull men ; but we knew them very well for all that, and we knew they were good men . . . Egerton, Gordon, young Matthews, Spenser, Smith, the bombing fellow, Tompkinson—all gone. . . .

So we were silent for a long minute, remembering those men, and Mrs. Harry stared into the fire. I wondered what she was thinking of, and I was sorry for her. For when Harry got up there was a look about him which I had seen before, though not for many months—not since the first days on the Somme. . . .

While I was groping after my coat in the hall, Harry came out of his den with a letter which he asked me to ' drop in the box.' I looked at it without shame ; it was addressed to Major Mackenzie, D.S.O., etc.

' And what have you said ? ' I asked.

' No,' said Harry, with a kind of challenging look.

' Well, I think you 're wrong——' I told him, though I knew then that I was too late. Mrs. Harry was beaten now, finally beaten, poor thing.

' And what are you two talking about ? ' said Mrs. Harry.

' About a dinner, my dear.'

I went out and posted that accursed letter, thanking God that I was not a wife.

XI

HARRY went to France again a month later, after the futile kind of medical examination which he had foretold. I had a letter from him from the Base, and after that there was silence. I even began to hunt about in the casualty lists, but he was never there. And seven weeks later they let me go out again myself, to the astonishment of all but the military doctors.

At the Base I heard of Harry. Some one had been wanted for some kind of job down there, an officer to instruct the Details in the mysteries of Iron Rations, or something of the sort. Harry, happening to be there at the time, and pleasing the eye of the aldermanic officer in command of our Base Depot, had been graciously appointed to the post. But he had caused a considerable flutter in the tents of the mighty by flatly declining it, and stating insanely that he preferred to go up to the line. This being still the one topic of conversation in the camp, I did not linger there longer than was absolutely necessary. Infantry Base Depots are bad places, and that one was very bad ; you had worse food, worse treatment, and worse company than you ever had in the line—much discomfort, and no dignity.   I never understood why officers should be treated with such contempt whenever there were a number of them together.   If you went about by yourself, or with another officer or two, you had a certain amount of politeness and consideration from military officials ; but as soon as you were with a ' herd ' of officers you were doomed—you were dirt.   If the intention at the Base was to make the line seem a haven of refuge and civility, it was highly successful as far as I was concerned.

I got back to the battalion under the usual conditions . . . a long jog in the mess-cart under the interminable dripping poplars, with a vile wind lashing the usual rain over the usual flat fields, where the old women laboured and stooped as usual, and took no notice of anything.   The heart sinks a little as you look at the shivering dreariness of it all.   And if it is near the line you hope secretly that the battalion is ' out ' for at least a few days more, that you may have just two days to grow used to this beastliness again, and not be met by some cheery acclimatized ass with a ' Glad to see you, old son—just in time—going up to-night, doing a " stunt " on Tuesday ! '   Yet, as you come to the village, there is a strange sense of home-coming that comes with the recognition of familiar things—limbers clattering and splashing along, and the regimental postman trudging back with the mail, and C Company cooker steaming pleasantly under an outhouse, and odd men with waterproof sheets draped over the shoulders, wet and glistening. To-day I was lucky, for the battalion was a long way back, resting, so that this home-coming sense was strong upon me. And I wanted to see Harry.

When I came near to the usual main street I saw the battalion marching in by a side road, coming back from a route march. I sent my gear ahead, and got down to see them pass. It was strangely pleasant. The drums of the little band were covered because of the wet, and only the bugles brayed harshly, but very cheerfully. Old Philpott was ahead of them, riding fatly on his mild black mare, and returned my salute quite amiably. I could see a lot of young recruits among the men, and there were many officers I had never seen, but the welcoming grins of the old men we had had from the beginning, mostly N.C.O.'s now, made up for that. Young Smith I saw, in command of C Company now, and Tarrant, our late Transport Officer, was squelching at the head of a platoon, obviously not liking it much. Then came D Company, and I looked eagerly for Harry. Stephenson I knew, in command (how young the company commanders were !), but

there were only two other officers, and they
both strange. The last of them tramped past,
and I was left silent in the rain, foolishly
disturbed. . . . Where was Harry ? Ass—no
doubt he is orderly officer, or away on a course.
But I *was* disturbed ; and the thought came to
me that if anything had happened to him I, too,
should be lonely here, with none of the Old
Crowd left.

I walked on then, and came to the little flag
of D Company headquarters flapping damply
outside an estaminet.   In the mess they greeted
me very kindly and gave me tea—but there was
still no Harry.   But they all talked very fast,
and the tea was good.

' And where's Penrose ? '   I asked at last.
' I haven't seen him yet ? '

I had spoken to Stephenson.   He did not
answer immediately ; but he picked up his
cup and drank, assiduously ; then he kind of
mumbled, very low and apologetic :

' He 's in his billet—under close arrest.'

' Under arrest !   My God, what for ? '

Stephenson began to drink again ; he was a
good fellow, who knew that Harry and I were
friends ; also he had known Harry in the
Souchez days, and he did not like having to tell
me this.

But one of his young subalterns, a young pup,
just out, was less sensitive, and told me, brutally:

'Running away—cowardice in the face of —*et cetera*—have some more tea?'

II

Bit by bit I heard the whole miserable story —or rather that naked kernel of it which passed publicly for the whole story. I had to make my own footnotes, my own queries.

The first night Harry was with the battalion Philpott had sent him up with a carrying-party to the front line, or thereabouts, fifty men and some engineering stuff of sorts, wiring trestles, barbed wire, or something. It was shell-hole country, no communication trenches or tracks, and since there had been an attack recently, the Boche artillery was very active on the roads and back areas. Also there was the usual rotten valley to cross, with the hell of a barrage in it. So much these young braves conceded. Harry had started off with his party, had called at the Brigade Dump, and picked up the stuff. Later on some one rang up Brigade from the line and said no party had arrived. Brigade rang up Philpott, and he sent up the Assistant Adjutant to investigate. Somewhere in the Arras Road he had come upon Harry, with most of the party, *running down the road—towards the Dump—away from the line*. The stores were urgently needed at the front; they never

got there.   That was all.   The court-martial was
to-morrow.

Well, it was a black story, but I made one or
two footnotes at once.

The very first night he was back!   The awful
luck—the cruelty of it !   Just back, in the
condition of nerves I knew him to be in, with
that first miserable feeling upon him, wondering
probably why the hell he had driven himself out
there, and praying to be let down easy for one
night at least—and then to be sent straight up
on a job like that, the job that had broken him
before.

And by Philpott !   I seemed to see Philpott
arranging that, with a kind of savage glee :
' Oh, here 's Master Penrose again—well, he 'd
better take that party to-night—instead of
Mr. Gibson. . . .'

And who was the Assistant Adjutant ?   God
knows, if every working-party that went wrong
meant a court-martial, there would be no
officers left in the army ; and if some busybody
had been at work. . . .

' Who 's the Assistant Adjutant ? ' I asked.

' Fellow who was attached to Division—used
to be in this battalion in your time, I believe—
what 's-his-name ? — Burnett — Burnett — he
rang up the Colonel and told him about it.'

Burnett !   I groaned.   The gods were against

Harry indeed. Burnett had been away from the battalion for eighteen months, drifting about from odd job to odd job—Town Major here, Dump Officer there, never in the line. . . . Why the devil had he come back now to put his foot in it—and, perhaps—— But I could not believe that.

Stephenson's two young officers—Wallace and Brown—made no footnote, naturally. They had come out by the same draft as Harry, one from Sandhurst, the other from a cadet school ; they were fresh, as Harry had been, and they had little mercy. And while I resented their tone, I tried to remember that they knew not Harry, and said nothing.

But when young Wallace summed up the subject with ' Well, all I can say is he 's a cold-footed swine, and deserves all he gets,' I exploded. ' You —— young pup ! ' I said. ' Just out, and hardly seen a shot fired—you dare to say anything about Penrose. I tell you you 're not fit to lick his boots. Do you know that he joined up in the ranks in August '14, and went through Gallipoli, and had done two years' active service before you even had a uniform ? Do you know he 's just refused a job at home in order to come out here, and another job at the Base ? Does that look like cold feet ? You wait till you 've been out a year, my son, before you talk about cold feet. You——' But I couldn't control myself any further. I went out, cursing.

III

Then I got leave to go and see Harry. He was in his billet, in a small bedroom on the ground floor. There was a sentry standing at the window, fixed bayonet and all, so that he should neither escape nor make away with himself.

He was surprised and, I think, really pleased to see me, for before me, as he said, or any one who knew his history, he was not ashamed. . . . It was only when the ignorant, the Wallaces, were near that he was filled with humiliation, because of the things he knew they were thinking. ' That sentry out there,' he told me, ' was in my platoon at Gallipoli—one of my old men ; just before you came in he tapped on the window and wished me luck ; he said that all the " old lads " did the same. . . . It bucked me up no end.'

Not that he needed much ' bucking up.' For he was strangely quiet and resigned—more nearly at peace with everything than I had seen him for many months. ' Only,' he said, ' I wish to God that I was a single man, and I wish to God they would get on with it. . . .' He had been under arrest for six weeks, six solid weeks . . . carted about from place to place like some animal waiting for slaughter ; while the Summaries of Evidence and the Memos and the Secret Envelopes went backwards and forwards through ' Units ' and through ' Formations,' from mandarin to mandarin, from big-wig to big-wig ; while generals, and legal advisers, and judge advocates, and twopenny-halfpenny clerks wrote their miserable initials on the dirty forms, and wondered what the devil they should decide—and decided—nothing at all. All this terrible time Harry had been writing to his wife, pretending that all was well with him, describing route marches and scenery, and all the usual stuff about weather and clothes and food. . . . Now at least somebody *had* decided, and Harry was almost happy. For it was an end of suspense. . . . ' Once they settled on a court-martial,' he said, ' I knew I was done . . . and except for Peggy, I don't care. . . . I don't know what they 've told you, but I 'd like you to know what really happened. I found the battalion at Monval (the same old part), and got there feeling pretty rotten. Old Philpott, of course, sent me off with a working-party like a shot out of a gun— before I 'd been there an hour. I picked up some wiring stuff at the Brigade Dump—it was a long way up the road then, not far from Hellfire Corner. Fritz was shelling the road like hell,

going up and down, dropping them in pairs,
fifty yards farther every time, *you* know the
game. . . . I had the wind-up pretty badly,
and so had the men, poor devils . . . but what
was worse, they seemed to know that I had.
. . . We had a lot of shells very close to us, and
some of the men kept rushing towards the bank
when they heard one coming. . . . Well, you
don't get on very fast at that rate, and it 's
damned hard to keep hold of them when they 're
like that. . . . And knowing they were like
that made me even worse. When we got to
Dead Mule Tree about ten of them were missing
. . . just stayed under the bank in the holes.
I don't say this to excuse myself . . . I
just tell you what happened. Then we got to
that high bit where the bank stops and the
valley goes up on the left. . . . You know
the awful *exposed* feeling one has there, and
they had a regular barrage just at the corner.
. . . I got the men under the bank, and waited
till a shell burst . . . and then tried to dash
them past before the next. But the next one
came too fast, and fell plunk into the middle
of the column—behind me. . . . Three men
were killed outright, and those of us who
hadn't flung themselves down were knocked
over. I fell in a kind of narrow ditch by the
road. When I put my head up and looked back
I saw some of the men vanishing back under

the bank. Then another one came—8-inch I should think they were—and I grovelled in the ditch again. . . . It was just like my awful dreams. . . . I must have been there about ten minutes. After every one I started to get up and go back to the men under the bank, meaning to get them together again. Every time the next one came too quick, and I was pinned, simply pinned in that ditch. Then Fritz stopped for a minute or two—altering the programme, I suppose—and I got up and ran like hell for the bank. The four or five men lying near me got up and ran too.

' When we got under the bank we lay down and I looked round . . . there was not a man to be seen. I shouted, but at first nothing happened. And, I tell you, I was glad. . . . Some of the men who had gone back, not seeing me anywhere, had melted away home. . . . I don't blame *them*. . . . Then a few drifted along from farther down the bank. . . . By degrees most of the party turned up . . . there must have been between thirty and forty of them in the end. . . .

' And then, you see, I knew I should have to go on again . . . get past the corner some-how. . . . And——

' And I couldn't. . . . I simply couldn't face it. . . . Peters (the N.C.O.) said something about " Going to have another shot, sir ? " He

was pretty shaken himself—they all were . . .
but he'd have gone. . . . We *ought* to have
gone on. . . . I know that. . . . But . . .
Anyhow, I told him I didn't think we should
ever get by at present, and said we 'd better go
back a bit and wait under cover . . . some yarn
or other. . . . So we started back down the
road. . . . The Boche was still doing the up
and down game on the road, only about twice
as much. . . . By this time I can tell you there
was no shame between those men and me . . .
we understood each other . . . every time we
heard that damned shriek we fell into shell-holes
and prayed. . . . They were following us down
the road, getting nearer and nearer. . . . You
know that dug-out in the bank where Headquarters used to be. Well, just when it looked
as if the next lot must come right on top of us,
I saw a light coming from the dug-out, and most
of us ran hell for leather for the door. Some
one was standing at the entrance as we dashed
in . . . just in time . . . we nearly knocked
him over. . . . And guess who it was,' said
Harry, with a horrible kind of hysterical laugh,
' guess who it was . . . it was Burnett—
Burnett of all people. . . . He had been sent
up to find out what had happened. Well, he
asked what the hell I was doing, and said I was
to go on at once. . . . I said I was going to
wait a bit, there was too much of a barrage. . . .

Then he said, very offensively, he couldn't help
that . . . my orders were to go on at once. . . .
That annoyed me, and I said I'd see him
damned first, and told him if it was so urgent
he could take the party up himself if he liked.
. . . But he didn't, naturally . . . no reason
why he should. . . . Then he rang up Philpott
and told him that he had seen the officer in
charge and some of the party *running down the
road—demoralized.* So he had, of course—he
saw me running for the dug-out . . . though
the joke of it is—the joke of it is . . . *he was
sheltering there himself!* ' And at the enormity
of that joke Harry went off into that hideous
laughter again. ' He said I refused to obey
orders, and asked for instructions. Philpott
said it was too late now, the stuff had been
wanted by midnight. . . . He told Burnett to
put me under arrest . . . and come back.

' That's what happened,' he went on, ' and
I don't care—only I wish it had been anybody
but Burnett—though I suppose he was quite
right ; but it makes no odds . . . I *had* got the
wind-up, and I *had* failed with the party, and I
don't deny it . . . even if I wasn't really
running when he saw me. . . . One thing I *can*
say—if I did have the wind-up I've never had
cold feet—till that night. . . . I'm glad I came
out this time if I did fail at the pinch. . . .
Burnett wouldn't have . . . I knew I was done

when I came . . . and I know I'm done now.

' But I wish you'd just explain it all to Peggy and the people who don't know.'

And that is what I am trying to do.

XII

THE Court-Martial was held in an old
farm lying just outside the village.
There was a large courtyard where the chickens
clucked all day, and children and cattle roamed
unchecked in the spacious midden. The court-
room was unusually suitable to its purpose,
being panelled all round in some dark wood with
great black beams under a whitewashed ceiling,
high and vaulted, and an open hearth where the
dry wood crackled heartlessly all day. Usually
these trials are conducted in the best bedroom
of some estaminet, and the Court sits defensively
with a vast white bed at their backs. But this
room was strangely dignified and legal : only at
first Madame persisted in marching through it
with saucepans to the kitchen—all these curious
English functions were the same to her, a
Christmas dinner, or a mess-meeting, or the
trial of a soldier for his life.

The Court impressed me rather favourably
—a Major-General, and four others. The
Major-General, who was President of the Court,
was a square, fatherly-looking person, with a
good moustache, and rather hard blue eyes.
He had many rows of ribbons, so many that as
I looked at them from a dark corner at the back,

they seemed like some regiment of coloured beetles, paraded in close column of companies. All these men were very excellently groomed : ' groomed ' is the right word, for indeed they suggested a number of well-fed horses ; all their skins were bright, and shiny, and well kept, and the leather of their Sam Brownes, and their field boots, and jingling spurs, and all their harness were beautiful and glistening in the firelight.   I once went over the royal stables at Madrid.   And when all these glossy creatures jingled heavily up to their table I was reminded of that.   They sat down and pawed the floor restively with their well-polished hoofs, cursing in their hearts because they had been brought so far ' to do some damned court-martial.'   But all their faces said, ' Thank God, at least I have had my oats to-day.'

And there was an atmosphere of greyness about them.   The hair of some of them was splashed with grey ; the faces of most of them were weathered and grey ; and one felt that the opinions of all of them were grey, but not weathered.

For they were just men, according to their views.   They would do the thing conscientiously and I could not have hoped for a better Court.   But as judges they held the fatal military heresy, that the forms and procedure of Military Law are the best conceivable

machinery for the discovery of truth. It was
not their fault; they had lived with it from
their youth. And since it is really a form of
conceit, the heresy had this extension, that they
themselves, and men like them, blunt, honest,
straightforward men, were the best conceivable
ministers for the discovery of truth—and they
needed no assistance. Any of them would have
told you, ' Damn it, sir, there's nothing fairer
to the prisoner than a Field General Court-
Martial'; and if you read the books or witness
the trial of a soldier for some simple ' crime,'
you will agree. But given a complex case,
where testimony is at all doubtful, where there
are cross-currents and hidden animosities, the
' blunt, honest ' men are lost.

To begin with, being in their own view all-
seeing and all-just, they consider the Prisoner's
Friend to be superfluous: and if he attempts
any genuine advocacy they cannot stomach the
sight of him. ' Prisoner's Friend be damned ! '
they will tell you, ' the Prosecutor does all that ;
and anything he doesn't find out the Court will.'
Now the Prosecutor is indeed charged with the
duty of ' bringing out anything in the favour
of the Accused ': that is to say, if Private
Smith after looting his neighbour becomes
afterwards remorseful and returns his loot to
its owner, the Prosecutor will ask questions to
establish the fact. In a case like Harry's it

means practically nothing.   The Prosecutor will
not cross-examine a shifty or suspicious witness
—dive into his motives—get at the secret
history of the business, first, because it is not
his job and secondly because, being as a rule
only the adjutant of his battalion, he does not
know how.

The Court will not do this, because they do
not know anything about the secret history, and
they are incapable of imagining any ; because
they believe implicitly that any witness, officer
or man (except perhaps the accused), is a blunt,
honest, straightforward man like themselves,
and incapable of deception or concealment.

This is the job of the Prisoner's Friend.   Now
' The Book ' lays down very fairly that if he be
an officer, or otherwise qualified, Prisoner's
Friend shall have all the rights of defending
counsel in a civil court.   In practice, the
' blunt men ' often make nothing of this safe-
guard.   Many courts I have been before had
never heard of the provision ; many, having
heard of it, refused flatly to recognize it, or
insisted that all questions should be put *through
them*.   When they do recognize the right, they
are immediately prejudiced against the prisoner
if that right is exercised.   Any attempt to
discredit or genuinely cross-examine a witness
is regarded as a rather sinister piece of ' cleverness ' ; and if the Prisoner's Friend ventures to

sum up the evidence in the accused's favour at the end—it is too often ' that damned lawyer-stuff.' Usually it is safer for a prisoner to abandon his rights altogether in that respect.

But that should not be in a case like Harry's. The question of counsel was vital in his case. I make no definite charges against Philpott and Burnett. All I say is that it was *unfortunate* that the two men most instrumental in bringing Harry to trial should have been the only two men with whom he had ever had any bitterness during his whole military career. It was specially unfortunate that Burnett should be the first and principal accuser, when you remembered that almost the last time Harry had seen Burnett he had shown courage where Burnett had shown cowardice, and thus humiliated him. This case could have been passed over ; hundreds such have been passed over, and on their merits, from any human standpoint, rightly. Why was this one dragged up and sent stinking to the mandarins ? Well, one possible answer was—' Look at the history of these three men.' And in the light of that history I say that Philpott and Burnett should have been ruthlessly cross-examined by a really able man, till the very heart of them both lay bare. Whether the issue would have been different I don't know, but at least there would have been some justice on both sides. And it

may even be that a trained lawyer could not
only have got at the heart of the matter, but
also prevailed upon the Court not to be prejudiced against him by his getting at it.   For that
brings you back to the real trouble.   I could
have done it myself and gladly ; if any one
knew anything about these men, I did.   But
if I, acting for Harry, had really cross-examined
Burnett, asked him suddenly what *he* was doing
in that dug-out, and when he hesitated,
suggested that he too was sheltering, and quite
rightly, because the fire was so heavy ; or if
I brought out the history of that night at
Gallipoli, and suggested that the animosity
between the two men might both explain
Harry's conduct in the dug-out, and account
for Burnett having made the charge in the first
place, thus throwing some doubt on the value
of his evidence—all that would have been
' cleverness.'   And if I had suggested that
Philpott himself, my C.O., might have some
slight spite against the accused, or asked him
why he had applied for a court-martial on this
case after hushing up so many worse ones, I
think the Court would have thought not better
of Harry, but worse.

Then again it had been fixed that Travers
should be Prisoner's Friend; he knew more
about the Papers and the Summary of Evidence,
and so on, than any one (though as the papers

had only been sent down the morning before, he did not know a great deal). So we left it at that. Travers was a young law student in private life, but constitutionally timid of authority, and he made no great show, in spite of the efforts of the Deputy Judge Advocate, a person supposed to assist everybody. But, as I have said, perhaps it was as well.

For what they thought of as the 'hard facts of the case' were all that mattered to the Court, and as related by Philpott and Burnett and Peters, they were pretty damning. That bit about the 'running' was fatal. It made a great impression. Both the Prosecutor and two of the Court asked Burnett, 'Are you sure he was *running*?' If he had only been *walking* away from the enemy it would have made so much difference!

Travers did ask Burnett why was he in the dug-out entrance; and it showed you what a mockery any kind of cross-examination would have been. In the absence of shorthand writers every question and almost every answer was written down, word for word, by the Deputy Judge Advocate. After a question was put there was a lengthy pause while the officer wrote; then there was some uncertainty and some questions about the exact form of the question. Had Travers said, 'Why were you in the dug-out?' or 'Why did you go to the dug-out ? ' Finally, all being satisfactorily settled and written down, the witness was allowed to answer. But by then the shiftiest witness had had time to invent a dozen suitable answers. No liar could possibly be caught out —no deceiver ever be detected—under this system. That was ' being fair to the witness.'

Burnett answered, of course, that he had gone there to inquire if the working-party had been seen.

To do Burnett justice, he did not seem at all happy at having to tell his tale again. If his original report had really been made under a sudden impulse of spite and revenge (and, however that may be, he could certainly have made a very different report), I think perhaps he had not realized how far the matter would go—had not imagined that it would come to a court-martial, and now regretted it. But it was too late. He could not eat his words. And that was the devil of it. Burnett might have made a different report ; Philpott could have ' arranged things ' with the Brigade—could have had Harry sent to the Base on the ground of his record and medical condition, and not have applied for a court-martial. But once those ' hard facts ' came before the Court, to be examined under that procedure, simply as ' hard facts '—an officer ordered up with a party and important stores ; some of the party

scattered; officer seen running—*running*, mind
you—in the wrong direction; officer ' shaken '
on the evidence of his men, and refusing to obey
an order—it was too late to wonder whether
the case should ever have come there. That
was Philpott's business. *He* did not seem
disturbed. He even mentioned—casually—that
' there had been a similar incident with this
officer once before, when his conduct with a
working-party by no means satisfied me.'
Quite apart from the monstrous misrepresen-
tation of the thing, the statement was wholly
inadmissible at that stage, and the President
stopped him. But that also was too late. It
had sunk in.

And so the evidence went slowly on, unshaken
—not that it was all unshakable ; no one tried
to shake it.

After Philpott came Peters, the N.C.O., a
good fellow.

He told the Court what Harry had said about
' going back to wait a bit,' instead of going
straight on when the party collected again.

They asked him, ' Was there any reason why
the party should not have gone on then ? '

' Well, sir,' he said, ' the shelling was bad,
and we should have had some casualties, but
I daresay we should have got through. I 've
seen as bad before.'

Then there was one of the men who had been

with Harry, a good fellow too, who hated being there. He told the story of the movements of the party with the usual broken irrelevance, but by his too obvious wish to help Harry did him no good. When asked ' in what condition ' the officer was, he said, ' Well, sir, he seemed to have lost his nerve, like . . . we all of us had as far as that goes, the shelling was that 'eavy.' But that was no defence for Harry.

Harry could either ' make a statement ' not on oath, or give evidence on oath and be cross-examined. He chose the latter—related simply the movements of the party and himself and did not deny any of the facts of which evidence had already been given.

' When you had collected the party under the bank by this corner you speak of,' said the President, ' why did you not then proceed with the party ? '

' I thought the shelling was too heavy, sir, just then ; I thought it would be better to go back and wait a bit where there was more cover till the shelling got less. . . .'

' But Sergeant Peters says the party would probably have got through ? '

' Yes, sir.'

' In view of the orders you had received, wouldn't it have been better to go straight on ? '

' I don't know, sir—perhaps it would.'

' Then why didn't you do that ? '

' At the time, sir, I thought it best to go back and wait.'

' And that was what you were doing when you were seen—er, running to the dug-out ? '

' Yes, sir.'

Well, the Court did not believe it, and I cannot blame them. For I knew that Harry was not being perfectly ingenuous. I knew that he *could* not have gone on. . . .

Yet it was a reasonable story. And if the Court had been able to imagine themselves in Harry's condition of mind and body, crouching in the wet dark under that bank, faint with weariness and fear, shaken with those blinding, tearing concussions, not knowing what they should do, or what they *could* do, perhaps they would have said in their hearts, ' I will believe that story.' But they could not imagine it. For they were naturally stout-hearted men, and they had not seen too much war. They were not young enough.

And, indeed, it was not their business to imagine that.

Another of the Court asked : ' Is it true to say, as Private Mallins said, that you had—ah —lost your nerve ? '

' Well, sir, I had the wind-up pretty badly ; one usually does at that corner—and I 've had too much of it.'

' I see.'

I wondered if he did see—if he had ever had 'too much of it.'

Harry said nothing about Burnett ; nothing about Philpott ; probably it would have done no good. And as he told me afterwards, ' The real charge was that I 'd lost my nerve—and so I had. And I don't want to wangle out of it like that.'

That was the end of it. They were kind enough, those grey men ; they did not like the job, and they wanted only to do their duty. But they conceived that their duty was ' laid down in The Book,' to look at the ' hard facts,' and no further. And the ' hard facts ' were very hard.

The Court was closed while they considered their verdict ; it was closed for forty minutes, and when it reopened they asked for evidence of character. And that meant that the verdict was ' Guilty.' On the only facts they had succeeded in discovering it could hardly have been anything else.

The Adjutant put in formal evidence of Harry's service, age, record, and so on ; and I was allowed to give evidence of character.

I told them simply the sort of fighting record he had, about Gallipoli, and the scouting, and the job he had refused in England.

I am glad to believe that I did him a little

good ; for that evening it got about somehow that he was recommended to mercy.

And perhaps they remembered that he was twenty-three.

XIII

THAT evening I sat in C Company mess
for an hour and talked with them about
the trial. They were very sad and upset at
this thing happening in the regiment, but they
were reasonable and generous, not like those
D Company pups, Wallace and the other. For
they were older men, and had nearly all been
out a long time. Only one of them annoyed me,
a fellow in the thirties, making a good income in
the City, who had only joined up just before he
had to under the Derby scheme, and had been
out a month. This fellow was very strong on
'the honour of the regiment'; and seemed to
think it desirable for that 'honour' that Harry
should be shot. Though how the honour of the
regiment would be thereby advanced, or what
right he had to speak for it, I could not discover.

But the others were sensible, balanced men,
and as perplexed and troubled as I. I had
been thinking over a thing that Harry had said
in his talk with me—'If I did have the wind-up
I've never had cold feet.' It is a pity one
cannot avoid these horrible terms, but one
cannot. I take it that 'wind-up'—whatever
the origin of that extraordinary expression may
be—signifies simply 'fear.' 'Cold feet' also

signifies fear, but, as I understand it, has an added implication in it of *base yielding* to that fear. I told them about this distinction of Harry's, and asked them what they thought.

'That's it,' said Smith, 'that's just the damned shame of the whole thing. There are lots of men who are simply terrified the whole time they're out, but just go on sticking it by sheer guts—will-power, or whatever you like— that's having the wind-up, and you can't prevent it. It just depends how you're made. I suppose there really are some people who don't feel fear at all—that fellow Drake, for example—though I'm not sure that there are many. Anyhow, if there are any they don't deserve much credit though they do get the V.C.'s. Then there are the people who feel fear like the rest of us, and don't make any effort to resist it, don't join up or come out, and when they have to, go back after three months with a blighty one, and get a job, and stay there——'

'And when they are here wangle out of all the dirty jobs,' put in Foster.

'Well, they're the people with " cold feet " if you like,' Smith went on, 'and as you say, Penrose has never been like that. Fellows like him keep on coming out time after time, getting worse wind-up every time, but simply kicking themselves out until they come out once too often, and stop one, or break up suddenly like Penrose, and——'

'And the question is—ought any man like that to be shot ? ' asked Foster.

'Ought any one who *volunteers* to fight for his bloody country be shot ? ' said another.

'Damn it, yes,' said Constable ; he was a square, hard-looking old boy, a promoted N.C.O., and a very useful officer. 'You must have some sort of standard—or where would the army be ? '

'I don't know,' said Foster, 'look at the Australians—they don't have a death-penalty, and I reckon they 're as good as us.'

'Yes, my son, perhaps that 's the reason '— this was old Constable again—'the average Australian is naturally a sight stouter-hearted than the average Englishman—they don't need it.'

'Then why the hell do they punish English- men worse than Australians, if they can't even be *expected* to do so well ? ' retorted Foster ; but this piece of dialectics was lost on Constable.

'Anyhow, I don't see that it need be such an absolute standard,' Smith began again, thoughtfully ; he was a thoughtful young fellow. 'They don't expect everybody to have equally strong arms or equally good brains ; and if a chap's legs or arms aren't strong enough for him to go on living in the

trenches they take him out of it (if he's lucky).
But every man's expected to have equally
strong nerves in all circumstances, and to *go
on having them* till he goes under ; and when
he goes under they don't consider how far his
nerves, or guts, or whatever you call it, were
as good as other people's.   Even if he had
nerves like a chicken to begin with he 's expected
to behave as a man with nerves like a lion or a
Drake would do. . . .'

'A man with nerves like a chicken is a
damned fool to go into the infantry at all,'
put in Williams—' the honour of the regiment '
person.

'Yes, but he may have had a will-power
like a lion, and simply made himself do it.'

'You 'd be all right, Smith,' somebody said,
' if you didn't use such long words ; what the
hell do you mean by an absolute standard ? '

'Sorry, George, I forgot you were so ignorant.
What I mean is this.   Take a case like Penrose's :
All they ask is, was he seen running the wrong
way, or not going the right way ?   If the
answer is Yes—the punishment is death, *et
cetera, et cetera*.   To begin with, as I said, they
don't consider whether he was *capable* physically
or mentally—I don't know which it is—of doing
the right thing.   And then there are lots of
other things which *we* know make one man more
" windy " than another, or windier to-day than

he was yesterday—things like being a married man, or having boils, or a bad cold, or being just physically weak, so that you get so exhausted you haven't got any strength left to resist your fears (I've had that feeling myself)— none of those things are considered *at all* at a court-martial—and I think they ought to be.

' No,' said Foster, ' they ought to be considered *before* they decide to have a court-martial at all. A case like Penrose's never ought to have got so far.'

' You 're right—I don't know why the devil it did.'

' After all,' said Williams, ' you 've got to consider the name of the regiment. What would happen——'

But I could not stand any more of that. ' I think Smith 's on the right line,' I said, ' though I don't know if it would ever be workable. There are, of course, lots of fellows who *feel* things far more than most of us, sensitive, imaginative fellows, like poor Penrose—and it must be hell for them. Of course there are some men like that with enormously strong wills who manage to stick it out as well as anybody, and do awfully well—I should think young Aston, for instance—and those I call the *really* brave men. Anyhow, if a man like that really does stick it as long as he can, I think

something ought to be done for him, though
I 'm damned if I know what. He oughtn't . . .'

'He oughtn't to be *allowed* to go on too
long—that 's what it comes to,' said Smith.

'Well, what do you want,' Foster asked,
'a kind of periodical Wind-up Examination ? '

'That 's the kind of thing, I suppose.   It
is a medical question, really.   Only the doctors
don't seem to recognize—or else they aren't
allowed to—any stage between absolute shell-
shock, with your legs flying in all directions,
and just ordinary skrim-shanking.'

'But, damn it, man,' Constable exploded,
'look at the skrim-shanking you 'll get if you
have that sort of thing.   You 'd have all the
mothers' darlings in the kingdom saying they 'd
had enough when they got to the Base.'

'Perhaps—no, I think that 's silly.   I don't
know what it is that gives you bad wind-up
after a long time out here, nerves or imagination or emotion or what, but it seems to me
the doctors ought to be able to test when a
man 's really had enough ; just as they tell
whether a man's knee or a man's heart are
really bad or not.   You 'd have to take his
record into account, of course. . . .'

'And you 'd have to make it a compulsory
test,' said Smith, 'because nowadays no one 's
going to go into a Board and say, " Look here,
doctor, I 've been out so long and I can't stand

any more." They 'd send you out in the next
draft ! '

' Compulsory both ways,' added Foster:
' when they 'd decided he 'd done enough, and
wasn't *safe* any longer, he oughtn't to be
allowed to do any more—because he 's dangerous
to himself and everybody else.'[1]

' As a matter of fact,' said Williams, ' that 's
what usually does happen, doesn't it ?   When
a chap gets down and out like that after a
decent spell of it, he usually gets a job at home—
instructor at the Depot, or something.'

' Yes, and then you get a fellow with the
devil of a conscience like Penrose—and you
have a nasty mess like this.'

' And what about the men ? ' asked Constable.   ' Are you going to have the same
thing for them ? '

' Certainly—only, thank God, there are not
so many of them who need it.   All that chat
you read about the " wonderful fatalism " of
the British soldier is so much bunkum.   It
simply means that most of them are not cursed
with an imagination, and so don't worry about
what 's coming.'

' That 's true ; you don't see many fatalists
in the middle of a big strafe.'

---

[1] It is only fair to say that, long after the supposed
date of this conversation, a system of sending ' war-
weary ' soldiers home for six months at a time was
instituted, though I doubt if Foster would have been
satisfied with that.

' Of course there *are* lots of them who *are* made like Penrose, and with a record like his, something——'

' And it's damned lucky for the British Army there are not more of them,' put in Constable.

' Certainly, but it's damned unlucky for them to be in the British Army—in the infantry, anyhow.'

' And what does that matter ? '

' Oh, well, you can take that line if you like— but it's a bit Prussian, isn't it ? '

' Prussia's winning this dirty war, anyhow, at present.'

So the talk rambled on, and we got no further, only most of us were in troubled agreement that something—perhaps many things—were wrong about the System, if this young volunteer after long fighting and suffering, was indeed to be shot like a traitor in the cold dawn.

Nine times out of ten, as Williams had said, we knew that it would not have happened, simply because nine men out of ten surrender in time. But ought the tenth case to be even remotely possible ? That was our doubt.

What exactly was wrong we could not pretend to say. It was not our business. But if this was the best the old men could do, we felt that we could help them a little. I give you this scrap of conversation only to show

the kind of feeling there was in the regiment
—because that is the surest test of the right-
ness of these things.

They were still at it when I left. And as I
went out wearily into the cold drizzle I heard
Foster summing up his views with : ' Well,
the whole thing 's damned awful. They 've
recommended him to mercy, haven't they ?
And I hope to God he gets it.'

II

But he got no mercy. The sentence was
confirmed by the higher authorities. I heard
afterwards that the officers of the Court-Martial
were amazed and horrified to hear it.

I cannot pretend to *know* what happened,
but from some experience of the military
hierarchy I can imagine. I can see those
papers, wrapped up in the blue form, with all
the right information beautifully inscribed in
the right spaces, very neat and precise, carefully sealed in the long envelopes, and sent
wandering up through the rarefied atmosphere
of the Higher Formations. Very early they
halt, at the Brigadier, or perhaps the Divisional
General, some one who thinks of himself as a
man of ' blood and iron.' He looks upon the
papers. He reads the evidence—very carefully. At the end he sees ' Recommended to

Mercy.'—' All very well, but we must make an example sometimes. Where 's that confidential memo. we had the other day ? That 's it, yes. " Officer who fails in his duty must be treated with the same severity as would be awarded to private in the same circumstances." Quite right too. Shan't approve recommendation to mercy. Just write on it, " See no reason why sentence should not be carried out," and I 'll sign it.' Or, more simply perhaps : ' Mercy ! mercy be damned ! Must make an example. I won't have any cold feet in my Command.' And so the blue form goes climbing on, burdened now with that fatal endorsement, labouring over ridge after ridge, and on each successive height the atmosphere becomes more rarefied (though the population is more numerous). And at long last it comes to some Olympian peak—I know not where—beyond which it may not go, where the air is so chill and the population so dense, that it is almost impossible to breathe. Yet here, I make no doubt, they look at the Blue Form very carefully and gravely, as becomes the High Gods. But in the end they shake their heads, a little sadly, maybe, and say, ' Ah, General B—— does not approve recommendation to mercy. He 's the man on the spot, he ought to know. *Must* support *him*. Sentence confirmed.'

Then the Blue Form climbs sadly down to the depths again, to the low regions where men feel fear.

.   .   .   .   .

The thing was done seven mornings later, in a little orchard behind the Casquettes' farm.

The Padre told me he stood up to them very bravely and quietly. Only he whispered to him, ' For God's sake make them be quick.' That is the worst torment of the soldier from beginning to end—the waiting.

He was shot by his own men, by men of D Company.

III

After three months I had some leave and visited Mrs. Harry. I had to. But I shall not distress you with an account of that interview. I will not even pretend that she was ' brave.' How could she be ? Only, when I had explained things to her as Harry had asked, she said : ' Somehow, that does make it easier for me—and I only wish—I wish you could tell everybody—what you have told me.'

And again I say, that is all I have tried to do. This book is not an attack on any person, on the death penalty, or on anything else, though if it makes people think about these things, so much the better. I think I believe in the death penalty—I do not know. But I did not believe in Harry being shot.

That is the gist of it ; that my friend Harry was shot for cowardice—and he was one of the bravest men I ever knew.